story
WARREN ELLIS

art
KEN MEYER JR.

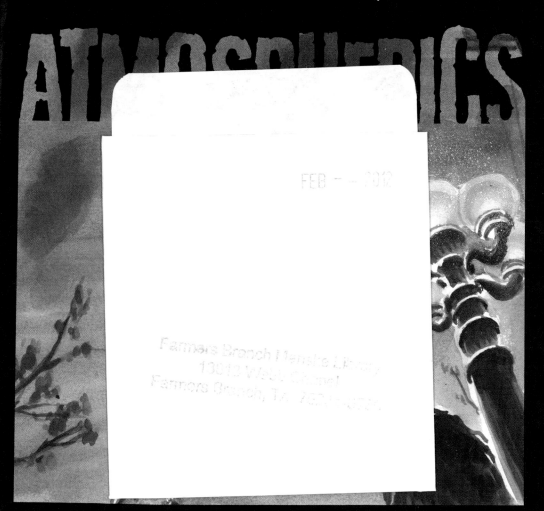

ATMOSPHERICS

WILLIAM CHRISTENSEN editor-in-chief   MARK SEIFERT creative director
JIM KUHORIC managing editor   KEITH DAVIDSEN director of sales & marketing
DAVID MARKS director of events   ARIANA OSBORNE production assistant

www.avatarpress.com   www.twitter.com/Avatarpress   www.facebook.com/avatarpresscomics

ATMOSPHERICS. First color printing December 2011. Published by Avatar Press, Inc., 515 N. Century Blvd. Rantoul, IL 61866. ©2011 Avatar Press, Inc. Atmospherics and all related properties TM & ©2011 Warren Ellis. All characters as depicted in this story are over the age of 18. Painted artwork TM & ©2011 Ken Meyer Jr. The stories, characters, and institutions mentioned in this magazine are entirely fictional. Printed in Canada.

AVATAR

ATMOSPHERICS

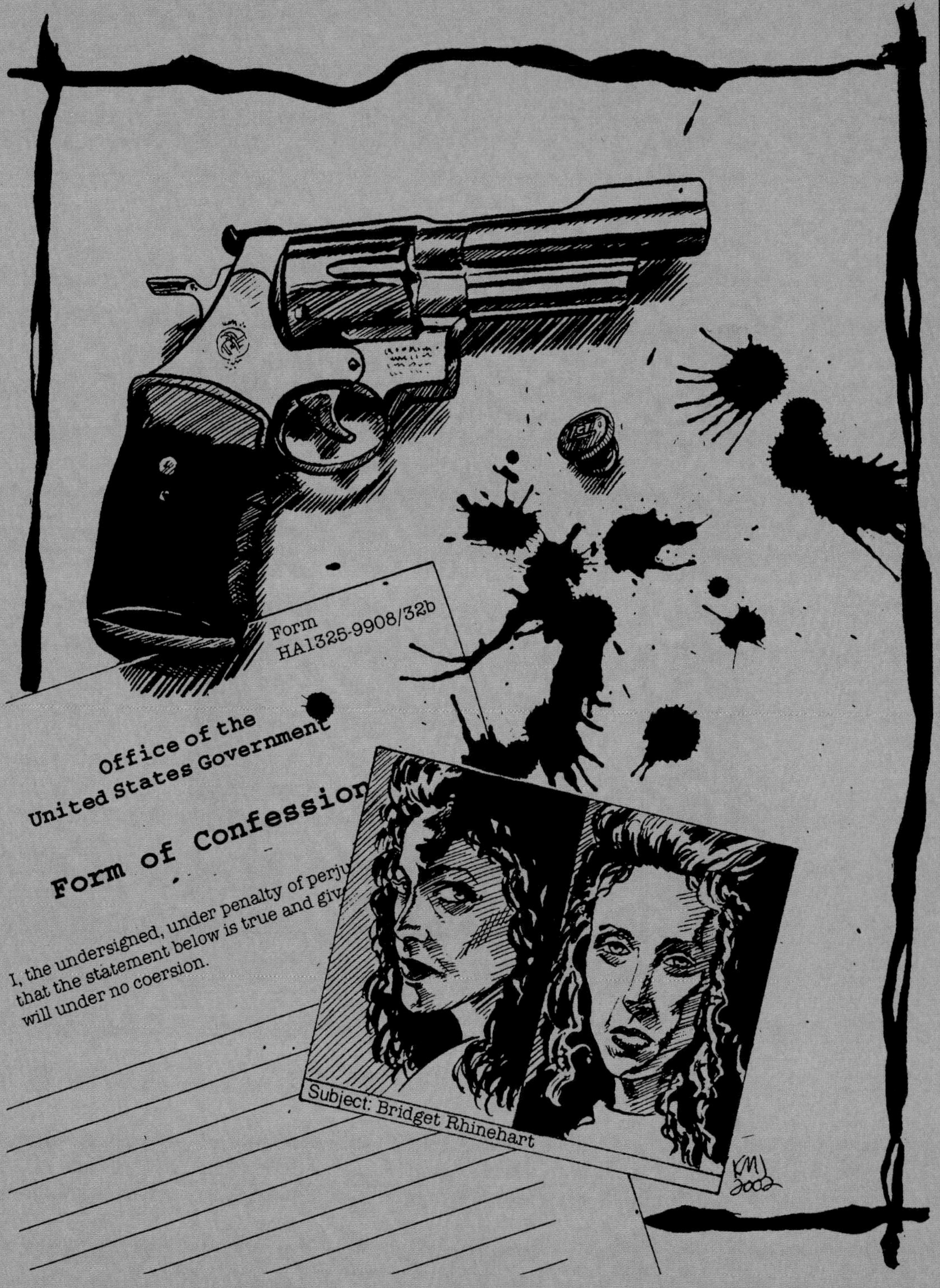
Form
HA1325-9908/32b
Office of the
United States Government
Form of Confession
I, the undersigned, under penalty of perju
that the statement below is true and giv
will under no coersion.
Subject: Bridget Rhinehart

Part One

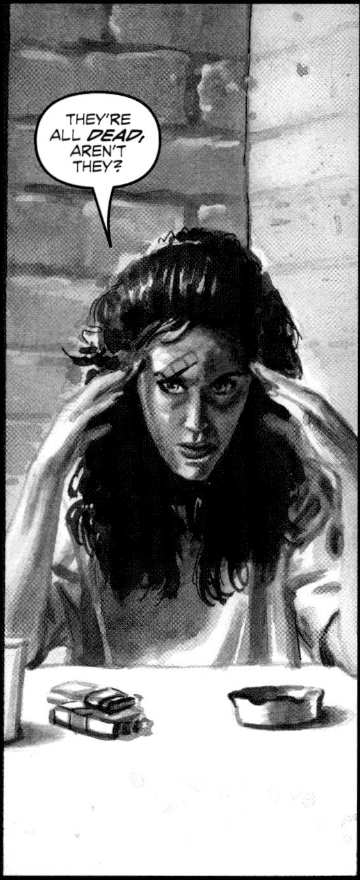
THEY'RE ALL *DEAD,* AREN'T THEY?

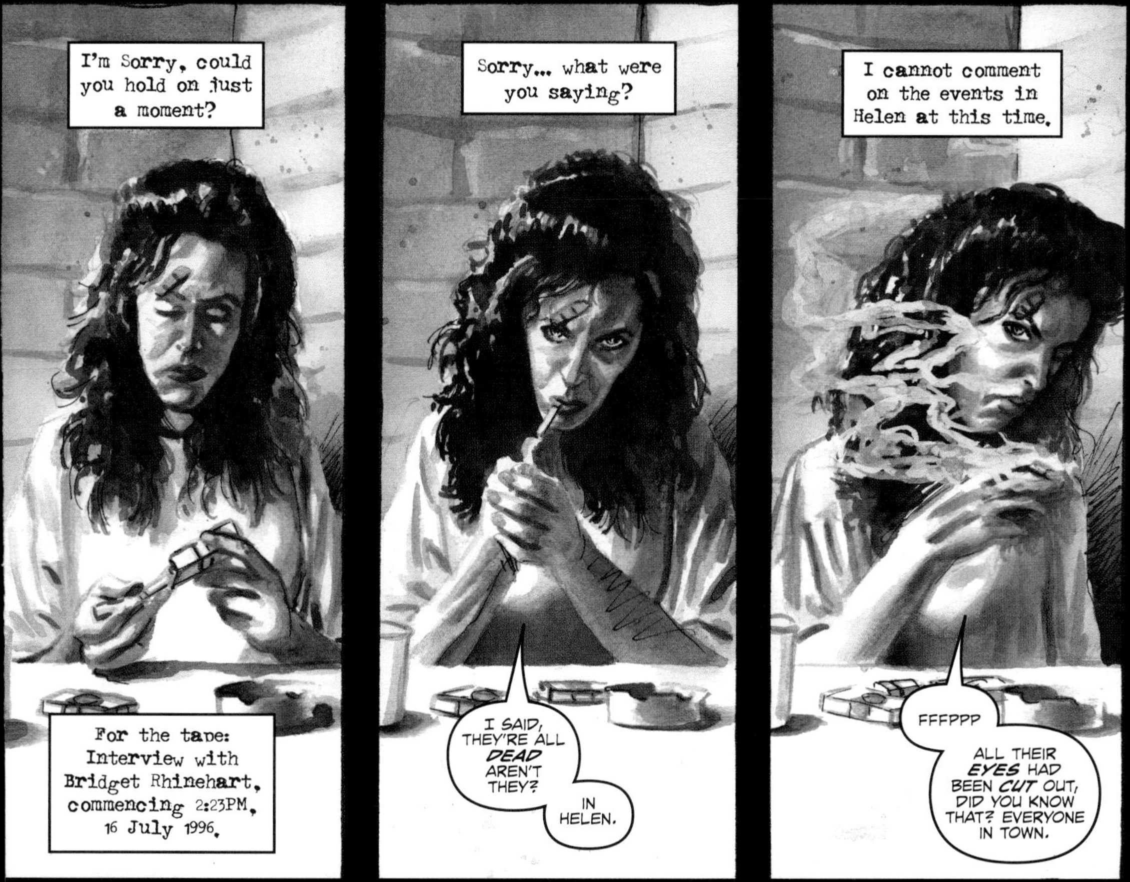
I'm Sorry, could you hold on just a moment?
For the tape: Interview with Bridget Rhinehart, commencing 2:23PM, 16 July 1996.
Sorry... what were you saying?
I SAID, THEY'RE ALL *DEAD* AREN'T THEY?
IN HELEN.
I cannot comment on the events in Helen at this time.
FFFPPP
ALL THEIR *EYES* HAD BEEN *CUT* OUT, DID YOU KNOW THAT? EVERYONE IN TOWN.

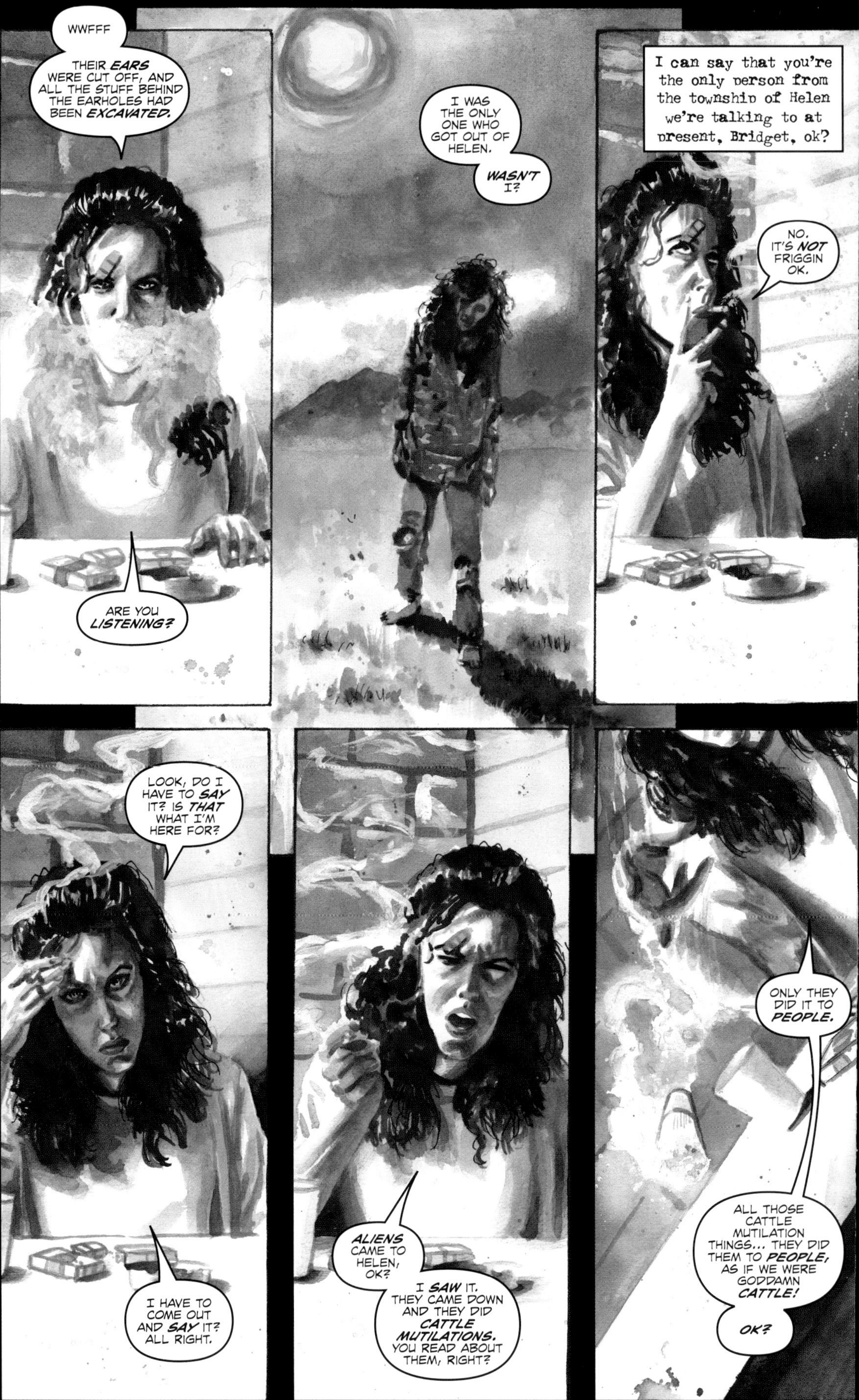
WWFFF
THEIR EARS WERE CUT OFF, AND ALL THE STUFF BEHIND THE EARHOLES HAD BEEN EXCAVATED.
ARE YOU LISTENING?
I WAS THE ONLY ONE WHO GOT OUT OF HELEN.
WASN'T I?
I can say that you're the only person from the township of Helen we're talking to at present, Bridget, ok?
NO. IT'S NOT FRIGGIN OK.
LOOK, DO I HAVE TO SAY IT? IS THAT WHAT I'M HERE FOR?
I HAVE TO COME OUT AND SAY IT? ALL RIGHT.
ALIENS CAME TO HELEN, OK?
I SAW IT. THEY CAME DOWN AND THEY DID CATTLE MUTILATIONS. YOU READ ABOUT THEM, RIGHT?
ONLY THEY DID IT TO PEOPLE.
ALL THOSE CATTLE MUTILATION THINGS... THEY DID THEM TO PEOPLE, AS IF WE WERE GODDAMN CATTLE!
OK?

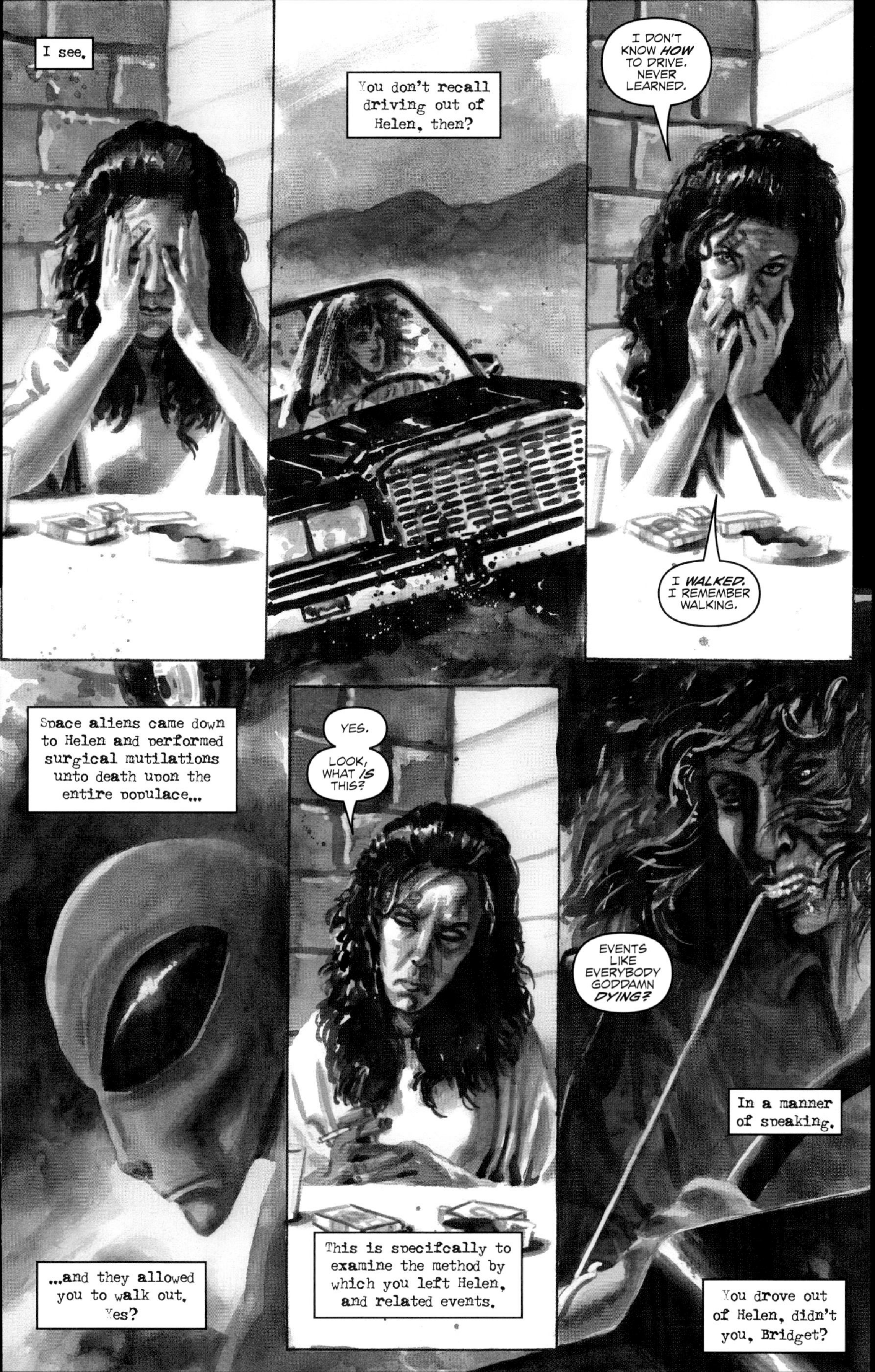

I see.
You don't recall driving out of Helen, then?
I DON'T KNOW *HOW* TO DRIVE. NEVER LEARNED.
I *WALKED.* I REMEMBER WALKING.
Space aliens came down to Helen and performed surgical mutilations unto death upon the entire populace...
...and they allowed you to walk out. Yes?
YES.
LOOK, WHAT *IS* THIS?
This is specifcally to examine the method by which you left Helen, and related events.
EVENTS LIKE EVERYBODY GODDAMN *DYING?*
In a manner of speaking.
You drove out of Helen, didn't you, Bridget?

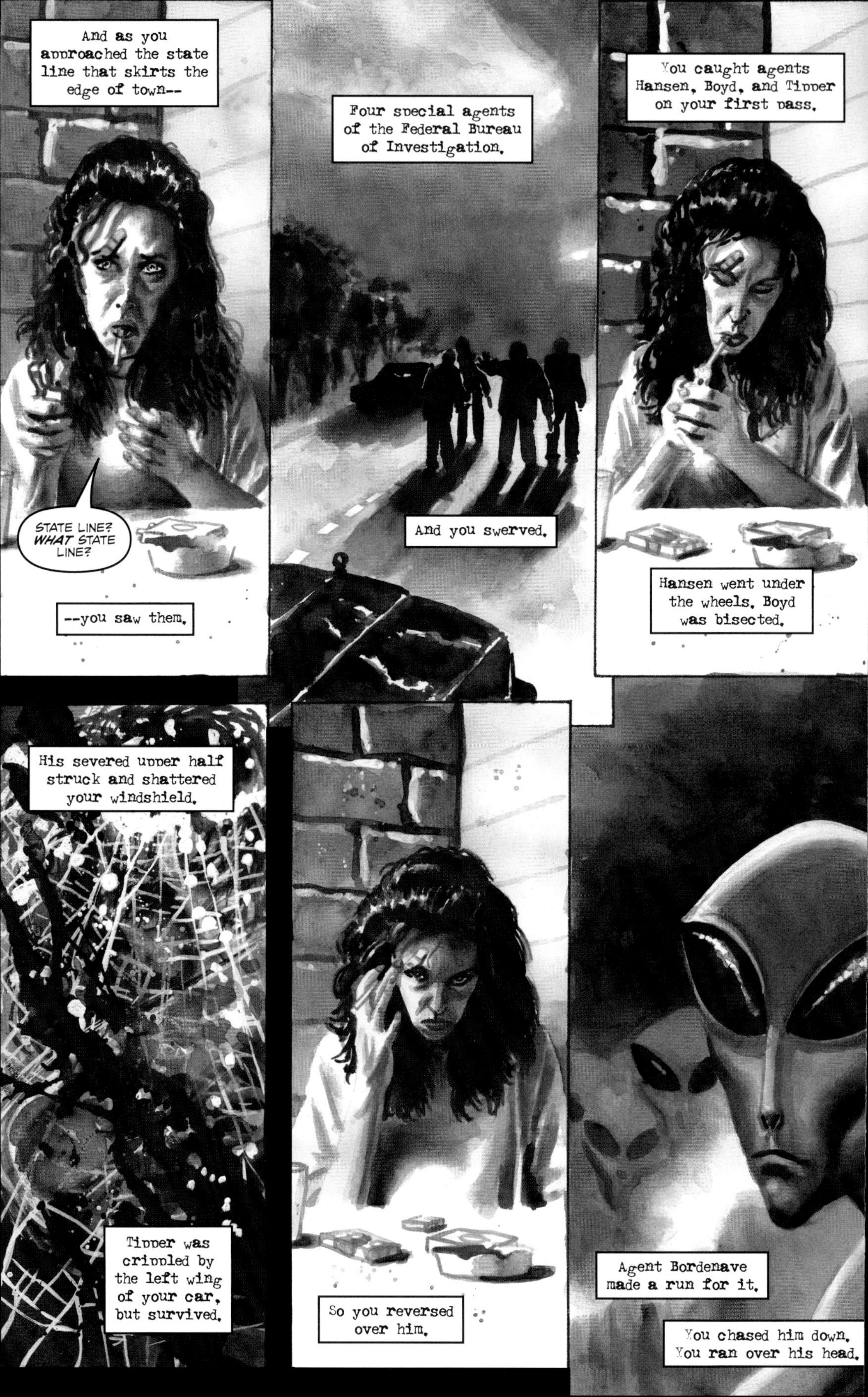
And as you approached the state line that skirts the edge of town--
STATE LINE? WHAT STATE LINE?
--you saw them.
Four special agents of the Federal Bureau of Investigation.
And you swerved.
You caught agents Hansen, Boyd, and Tipper on your first pass.
Hansen went under the wheels. Boyd was bisected.
His severed upper half struck and shattered your windshield.
Tipper was crippled by the left wing of your car, but survived.
So you reversed over him.
Agent Bordenave made a run for it.
You chased him down. You ran over his head.

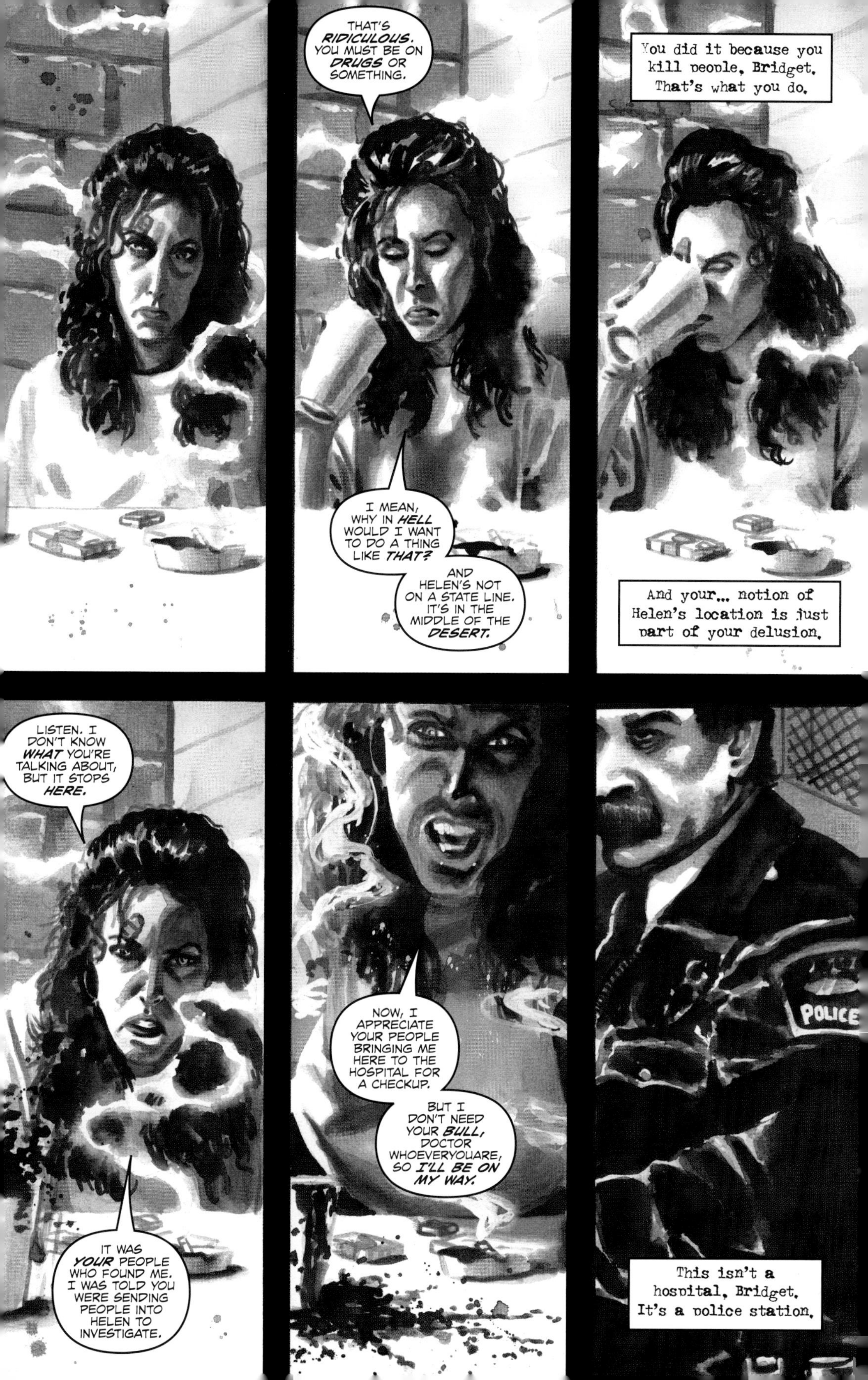
THAT'S RIDICULOUS. YOU MUST BE ON DRUGS OR SOMETHING.
I MEAN, WHY IN HELL WOULD I WANT TO DO A THING LIKE THAT?
AND HELEN'S NOT ON A STATE LINE. IT'S IN THE MIDDLE OF THE DESERT.
You did it because you kill people, Bridget. That's what you do.
And your... notion of Helen's location is just part of your delusion.
LISTEN. I DON'T KNOW WHAT YOU'RE TALKING ABOUT, BUT IT STOPS HERE.
IT WAS YOUR PEOPLE WHO FOUND ME. I WAS TOLD YOU WERE SENDING PEOPLE INTO HELEN TO INVESTIGATE.
NOW, I APPRECIATE YOUR PEOPLE BRINGING ME HERE TO THE HOSPITAL FOR A CHECKUP.
BUT I DON'T NEED YOUR BULL, DOCTOR WHOEVERYOUARE, SO I'LL BE ON MY WAY.
POLICE
This isn't a hospital, Bridget. It's a police station.

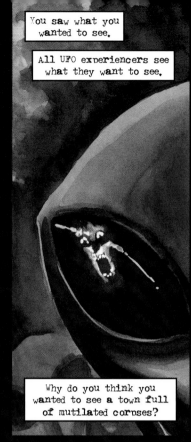

THIS IS *INSANE*.

I SAW DOCTORS, NURSES, BEDS, TROLLEYS...

You saw what you wanted to see.

All UFO experiencers see what they want to see.

OH BECAUSE I'M *HANNIBAL LECTER* IN BAD DRAG, *OBVIOUSLY*. I HAD A BOTTLE OF CHIANTI IN THE CAR I DON'T *DRIVE*.

Why do you think you wanted to see a town full of mutilated corpses?

YOU CAN'T MAKE IT *UNHAPPEN*, YOU KNOW.

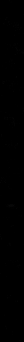

NOT SOMETHING LIKE *THAT*. THAT'S SOMETHING YOU DON'T *HIDE*; YOU DON'T *FORGET*.

YOU CAN'T *CONFUSE* ME INTO NOT REMEMBERING HOW THEIR BODIES *SPLIT OPEN*, HOW THEY SOUNDED WHEN THEY *RIPPED*...

Well, we'll see what you remember, and what you think you remember...

...once the interrogational drugs we placed in your coffee take effect.

WHAT DID YOU SAY?

Part Two

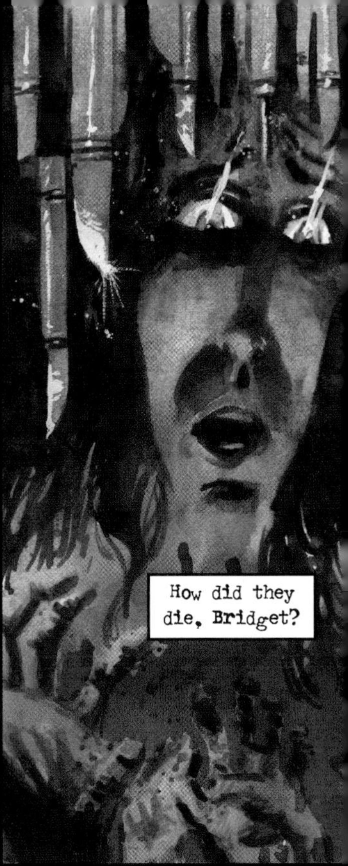
How did they die, Bridget?

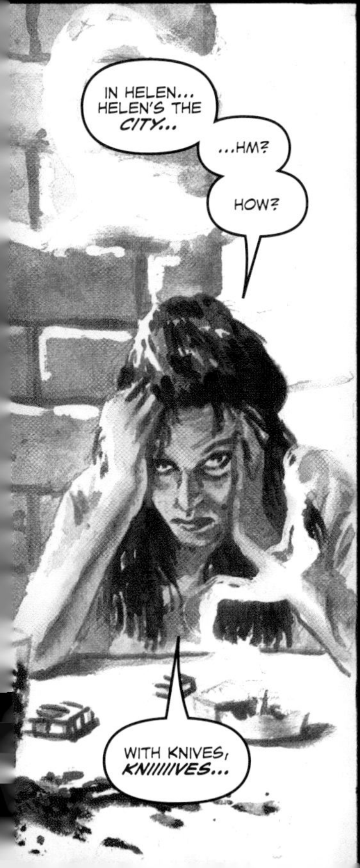
IN HELEN... HELEN'S THE CITY...
...HM?
HOW?
WITH KNIVES, KNIIIIIVES...

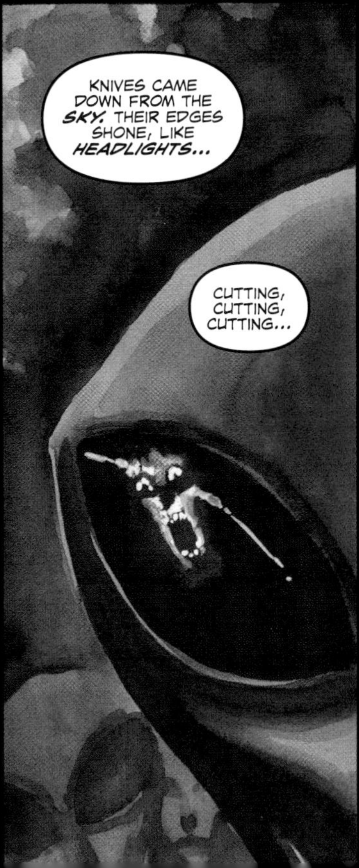
KNIVES CAME DOWN FROM THE SKY. THEIR EDGES SHONE, LIKE HEADLIGHTS...
CUTTING, CUTTING, CUTTING...

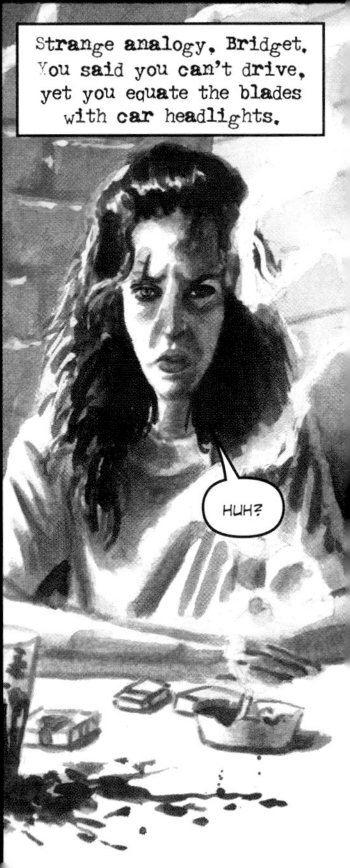
Strange analogy, Bridget. You said you can't drive, yet you equate the blades with car headlights.
HUH?

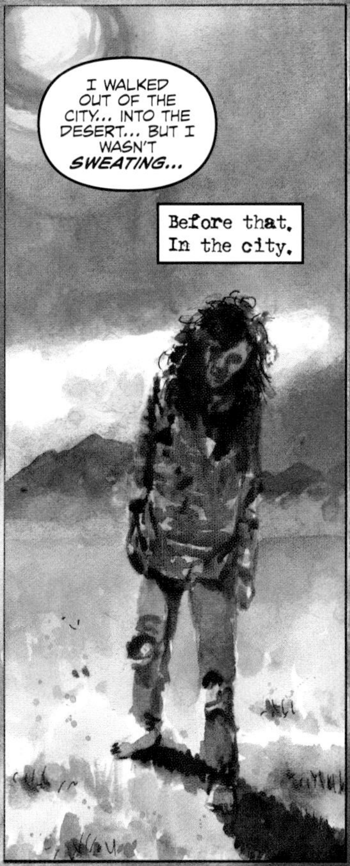
I WALKED OUT OF THE CITY... INTO THE DESERT... BUT I WASN'T SWEATING...
Before that. In the city.

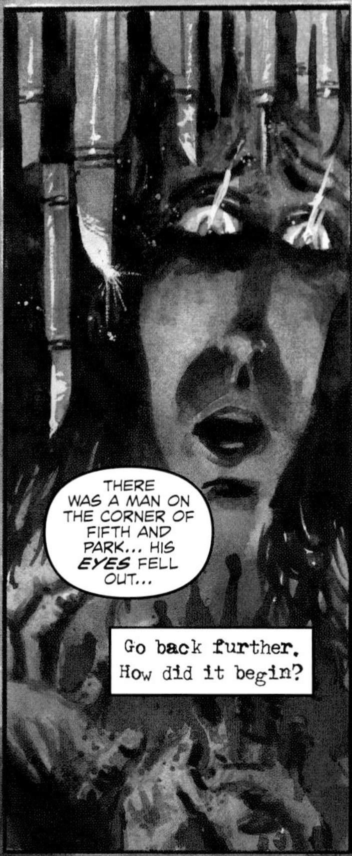
THERE WAS A MAN ON THE CORNER OF FIFTH AND PARK... HIS EYES FELL OUT...
Go back further. How did it begin?

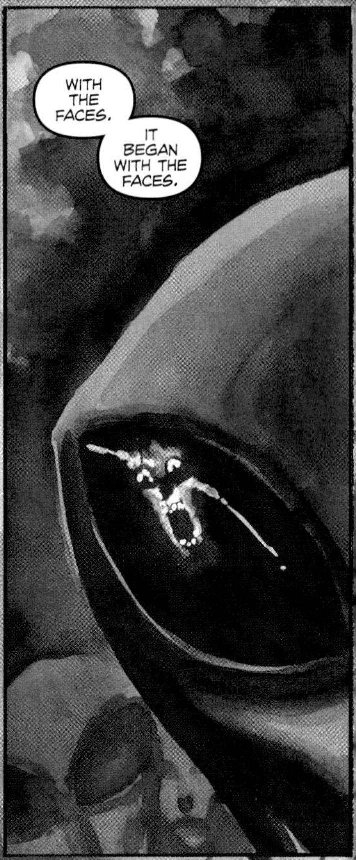
WITH THE FACES.
IT BEGAN WITH THE FACES.

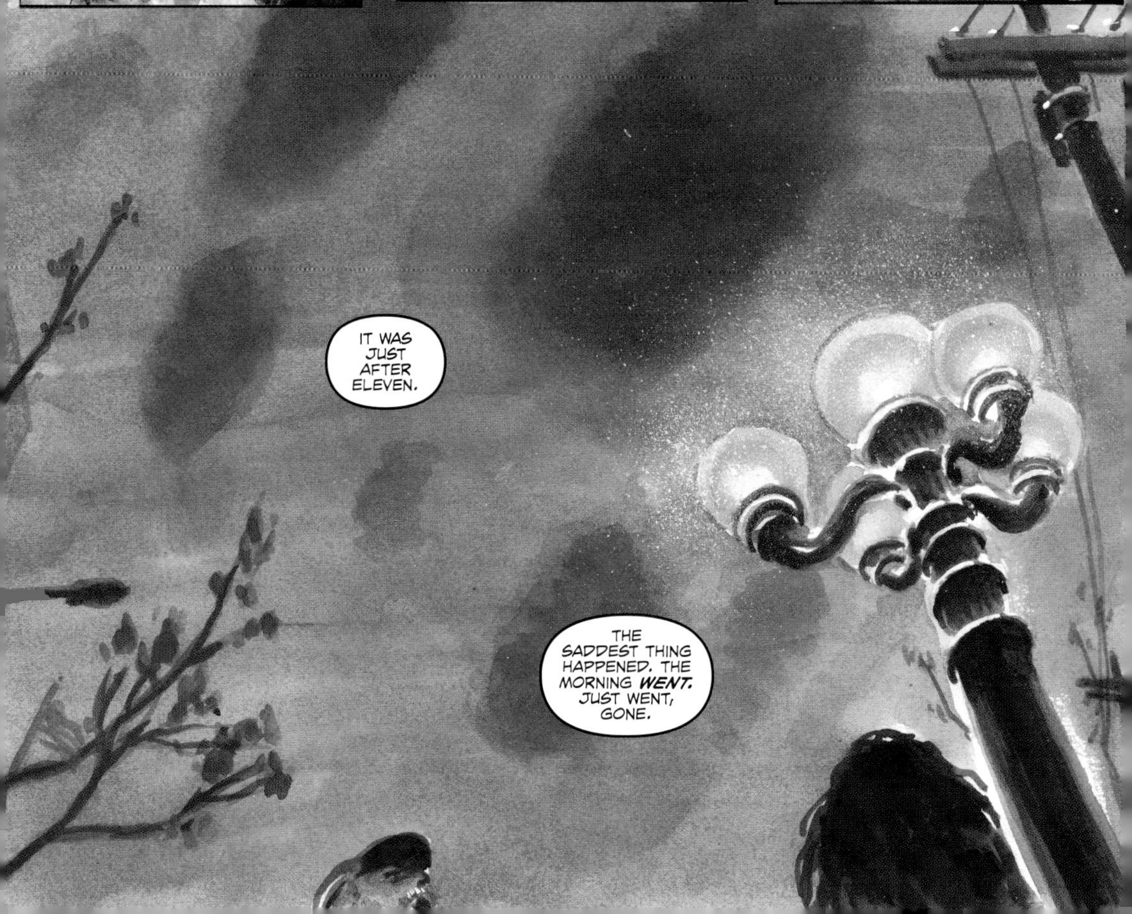
IT WAS JUST AFTER ELEVEN.
THE SADDEST THING HAPPENED. THE MORNING WENT. JUST WENT, GONE.

1
Extraction of ocular tissue
flesh and lips excised around the mandibles
tongue extracted/mouth cavity emptied
2
auditive internal and external organs extracted
cranial penetration—neural matter extracted?

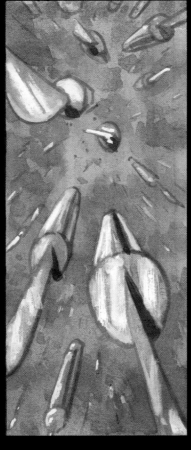

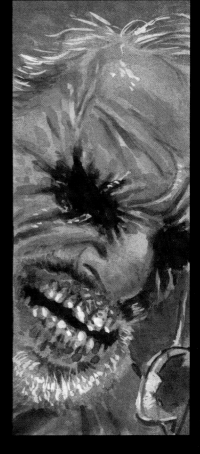

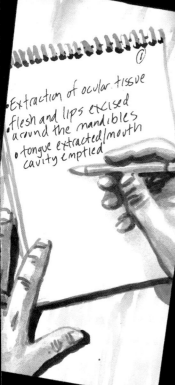

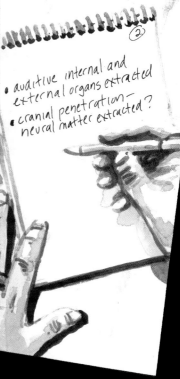

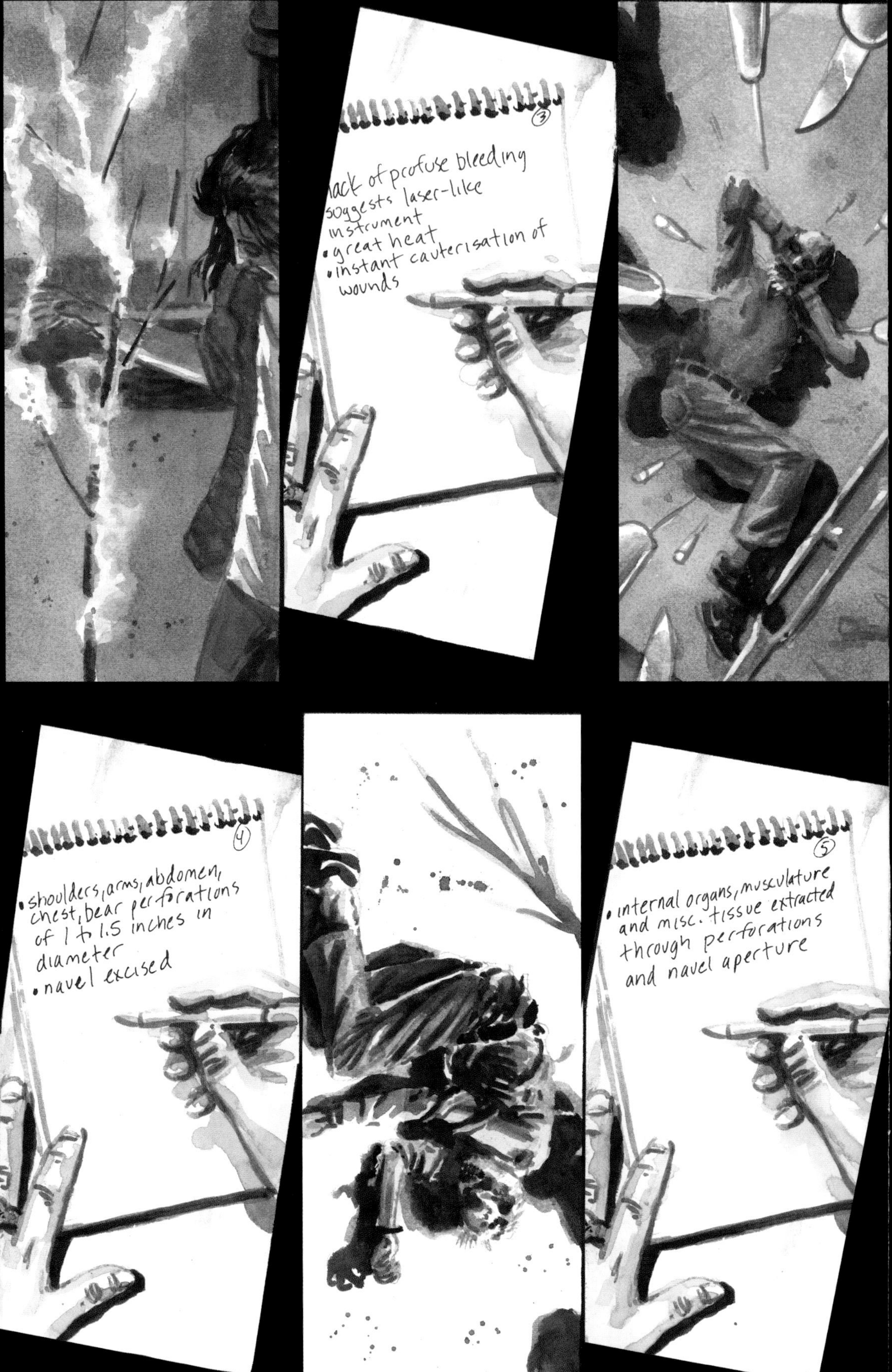
3
lack of profuse bleeding
suggests laser-like
instrument
• great heat
• instant cauterisation of
wounds
4
• shoulders, arms, abdomen,
chest, bear perforations
of 1 to 1.5 inches in
diameter
• navel excised
5
• internal organs, musculature
and misc. tissue extracted
through perforations
and navel aperture

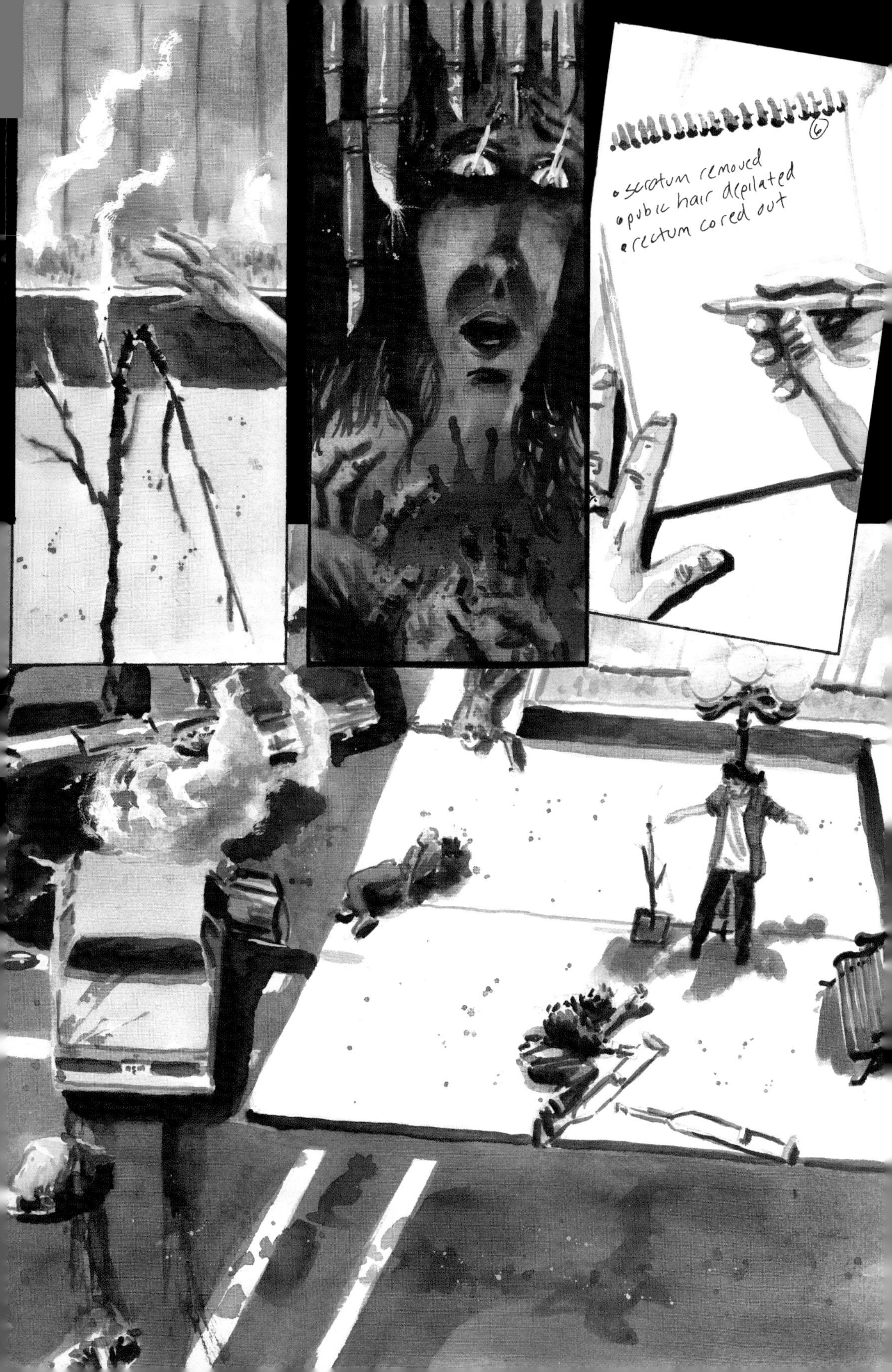
6
• scrotum removed
• pubic hair depilated
• rectum cored out

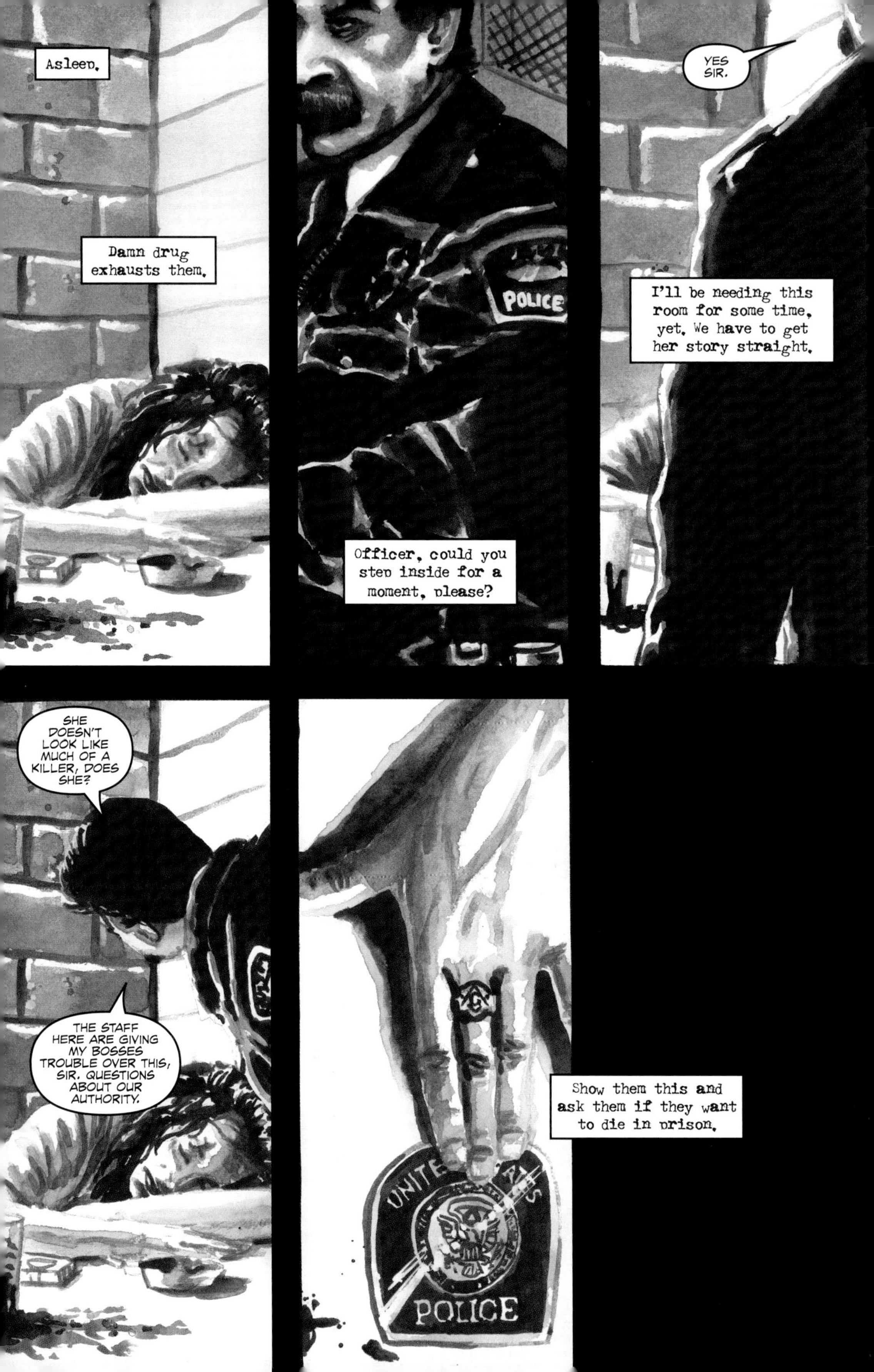

Asleep.
Damn drug exhausts them.
Officer, could you step inside for a moment, please?
YES SIR.
I'll be needing this room for some time, yet. We have to get her story straight.
SHE DOESN'T LOOK LIKE MUCH OF A KILLER, DOES SHE?
THE STAFF HERE ARE GIVING MY BOSSES TROUBLE OVER THIS, SIR. QUESTIONS ABOUT OUR AUTHORITY.
Show them this and ask them if they want to die in prison.
POLICE

Part Three

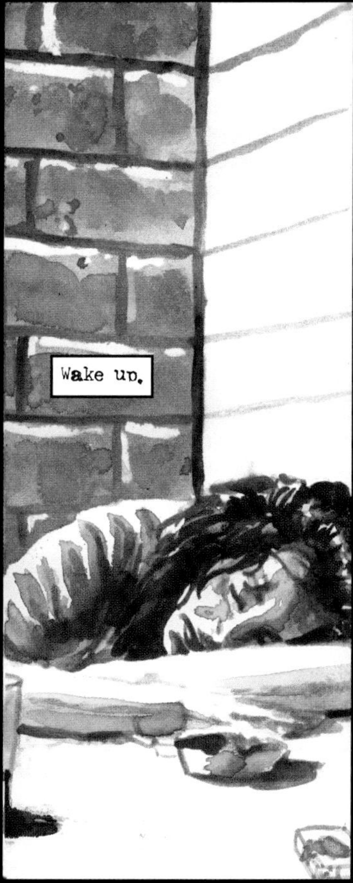
Wake up.

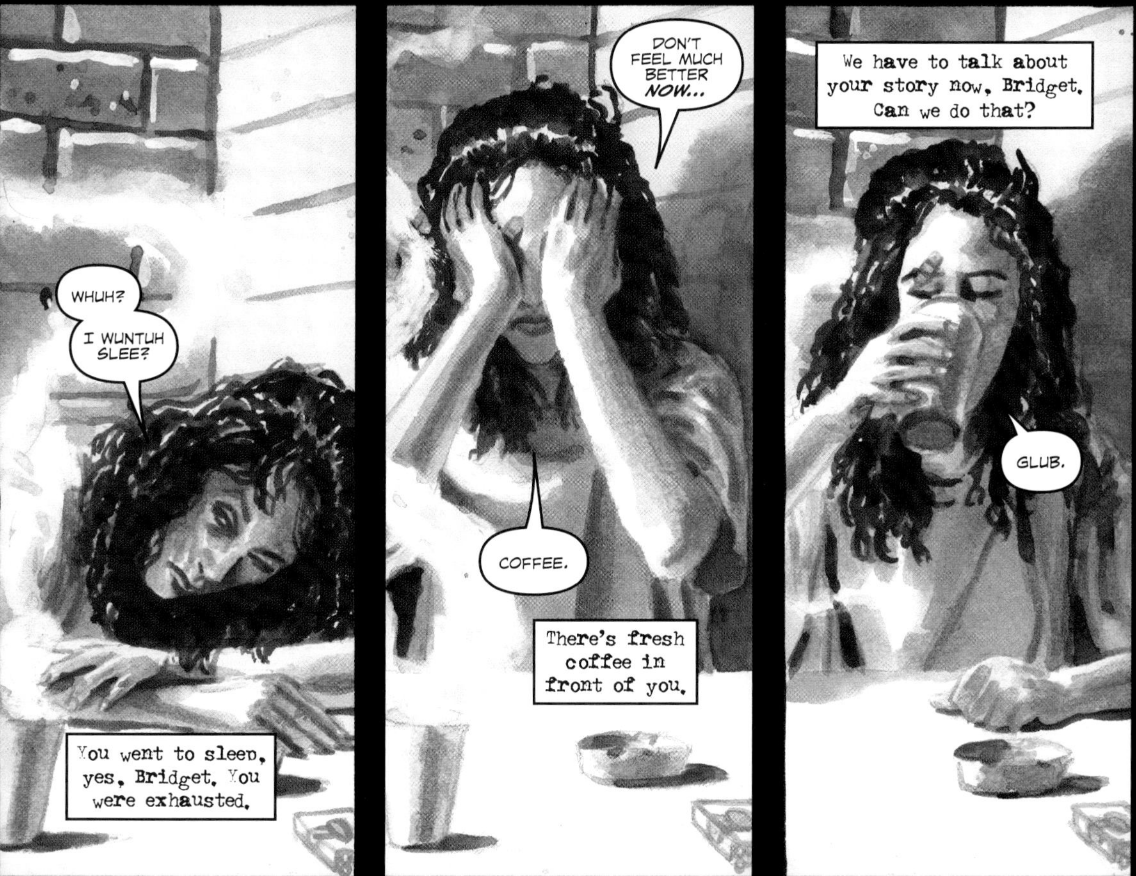
WHUH?
I WUNTUH SLEE?
You went to sleep, yes, Bridget. You were exhausted.
DON'T FEEL MUCH BETTER NOW...
COFFEE.
There's fresh coffee in front of you.
We have to talk about your story now, Bridget. Can we do that?
GLUB.

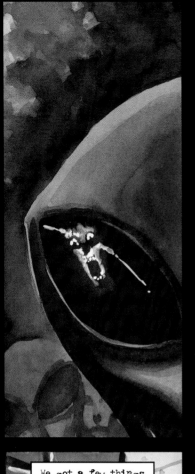

DRUGS.

YOU PUT DRUGS IN MY *COFFEE. THAT'S* WHY I PASSED OUT.

BASTARD.

WHAT DID I *SAY?* WHAT DID I *TELL* YOU?

WHAT DID YOU *DO* TO ME?

We got a few things straight, that's all.

Your cover story, for instance.

The one about the aliens mutilating the denizens of the township of Helen.

The one where you walk out of Helen alone and unmolested by said aliens.

Bridget, we've established that you're a drug addict.

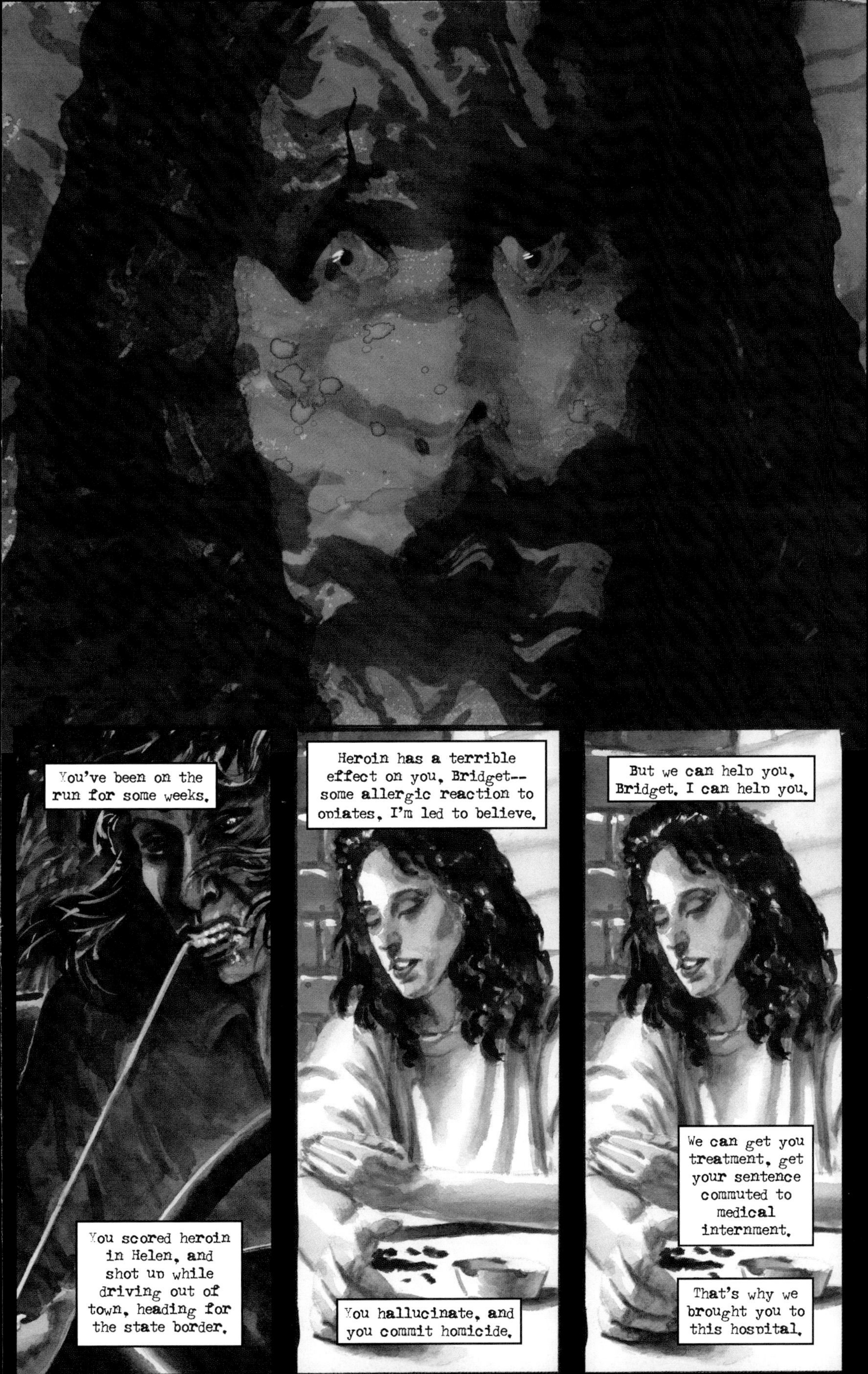
You've been on the run for some weeks.
You scored heroin in Helen, and shot up while driving out of town, heading for the state border.
Heroin has a terrible effect on you, Bridget--some allergic reaction to opiates, I'm led to believe.
You hallucinate, and you commit homicide.
But we can help you, Bridget. I can help you.
We can get you treatment, get your sentence commuted to medical internment.
That's why we brought you to this hospital.

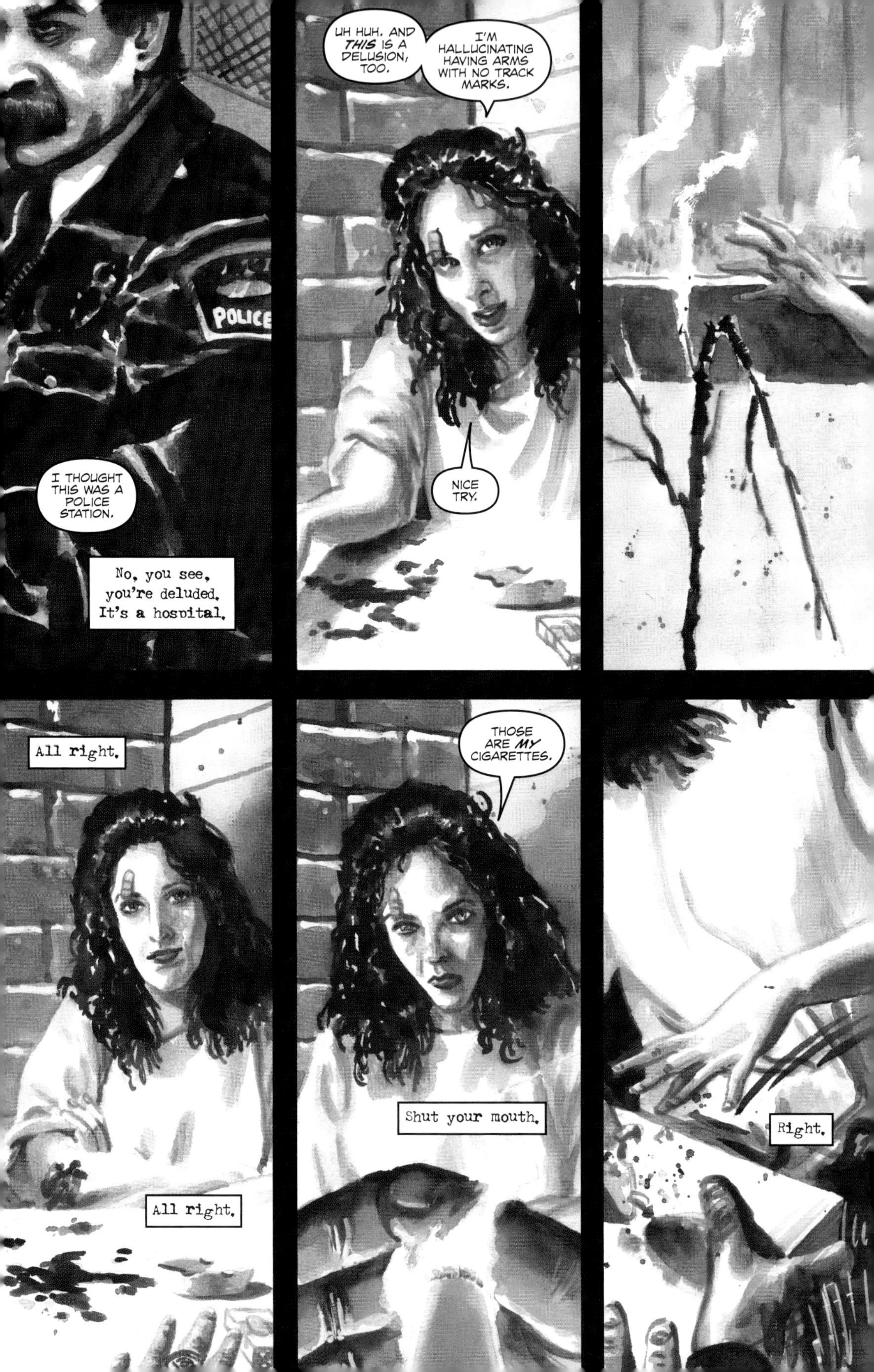
I THOUGHT THIS WAS A POLICE STATION.
No, you see, you're deluded. It's a hospital.
UH HUH. AND THIS IS A DELUSION, TOO.
I'M HALLUCINATING HAVING ARMS WITH NO TRACK MARKS.
NICE TRY.
All right.
All right.
THOSE ARE MY CIGARETTES.
Shut your mouth.
Right.

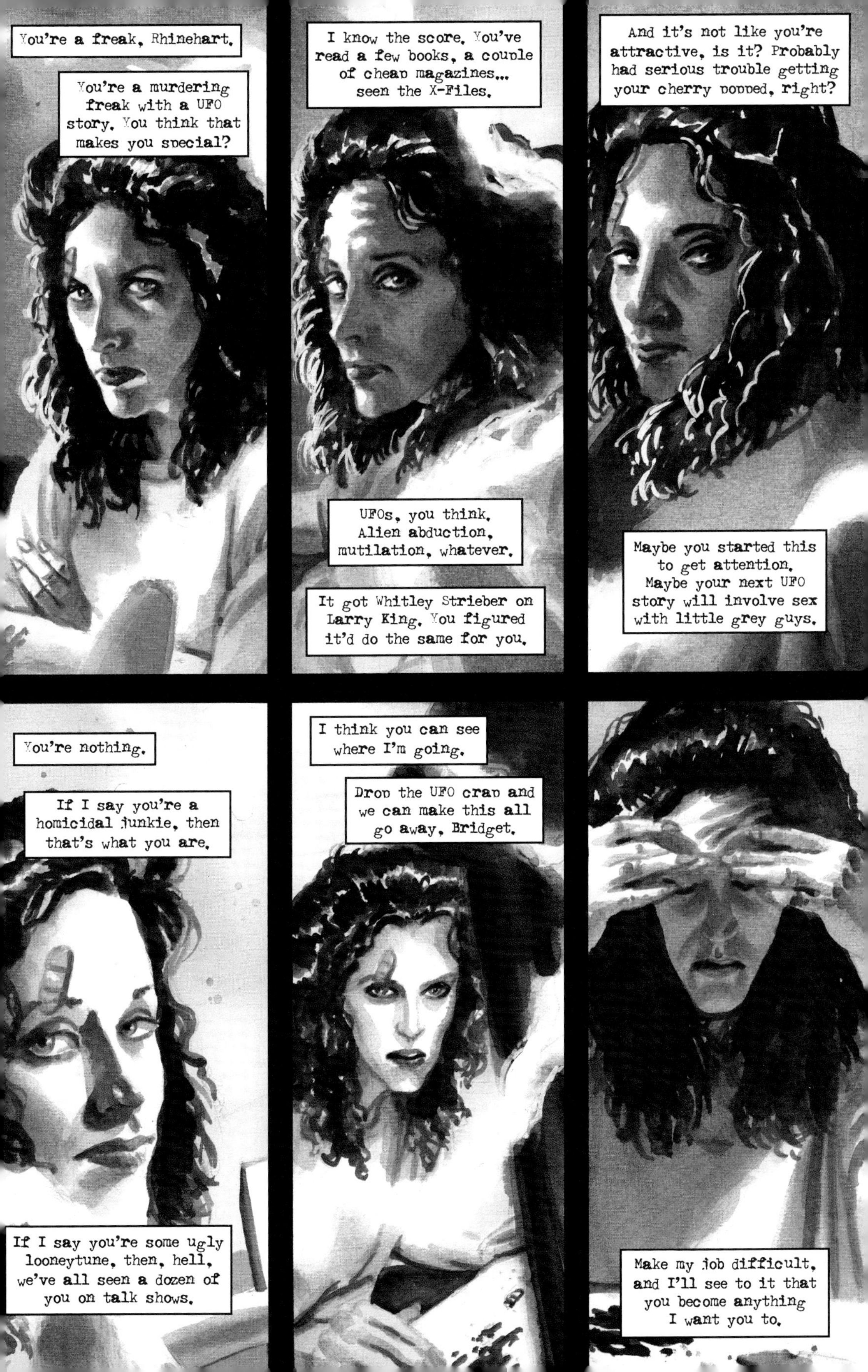
You're a freak, Rhinehart.
You're a murdering freak with a UFO story. You think that makes you special?
I know the score. You've read a few books, a couple of cheap magazines... seen the X-Files.
UFOs, you think. Alien abduction, mutilation, whatever.
It got Whitley Strieber on Larry King. You figured it'd do the same for you.
And it's not like you're attractive, is it? Probably had serious trouble getting your cherry popped, right?
Maybe you started this to get attention. Maybe your next UFO story will involve sex with little grey guys.
You're nothing.
If I say you're a homicidal junkie, then that's what you are.
If I say you're some ugly looneytune, then, hell, we've all seen a dozen of you on talk shows.
I think you can see where I'm going.
Drop the UFO crap and we can make this all go away, Bridget.
Make my job difficult, and I'll see to it that you become anything I want you to.

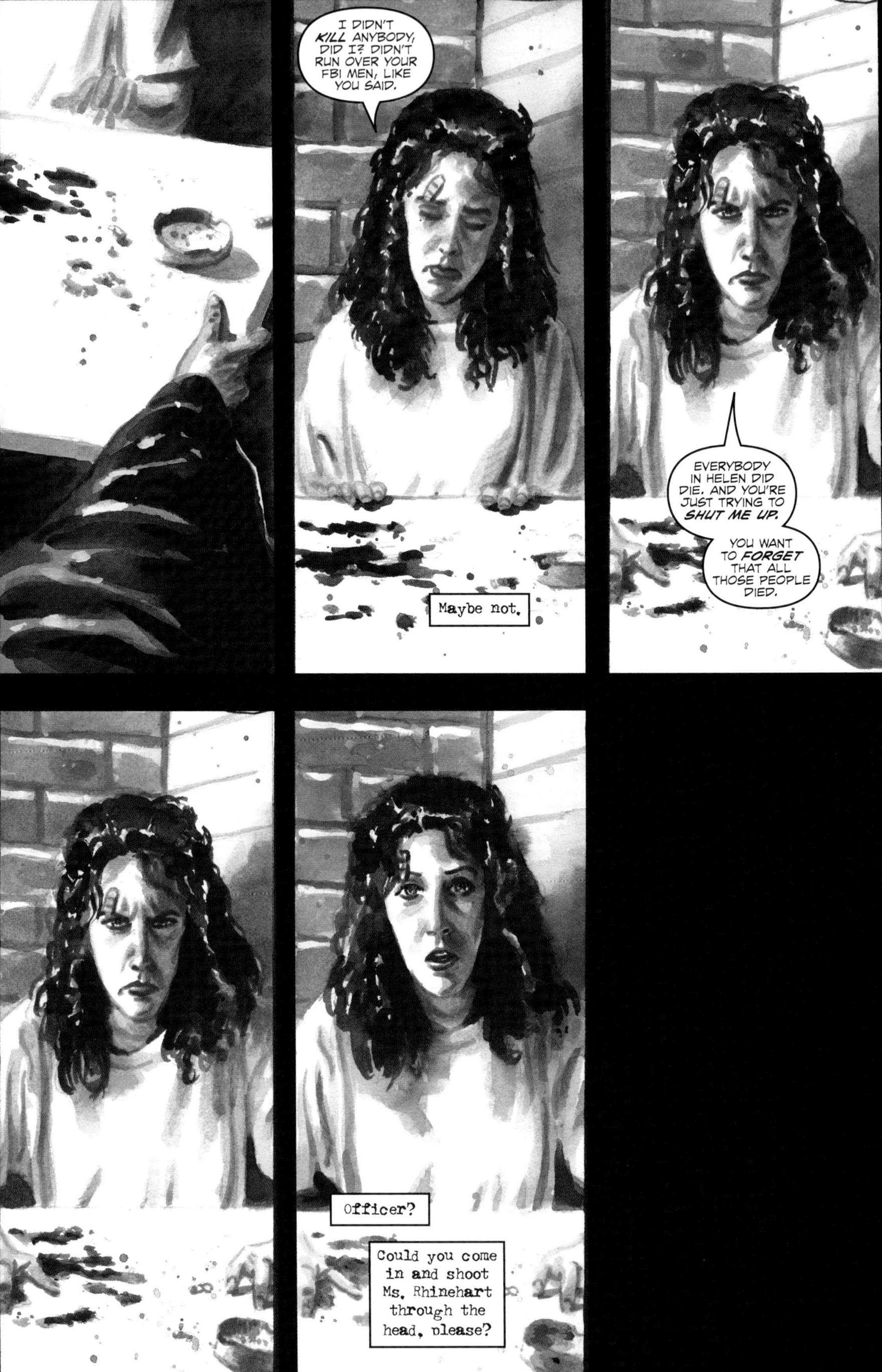
I DIDN'T KILL ANYBODY, DID I? DIDN'T RUN OVER YOUR FBI MEN, LIKE YOU SAID.
Maybe not.
EVERYBODY IN HELEN DID DIE. AND YOU'RE JUST TRYING TO SHUT ME UP.
YOU WANT TO FORGET THAT ALL THOSE PEOPLE DIED.
Officer?
Could you come in and shoot Ms. Rhinehart through the head, please?

Part Four

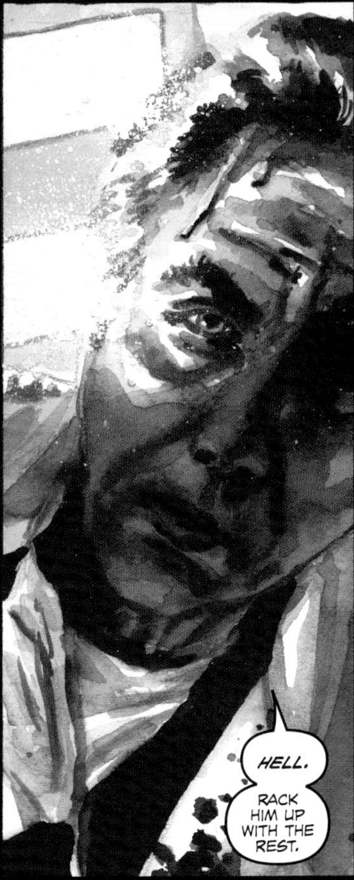
HELL.
RACK HIM UP WITH THE REST.

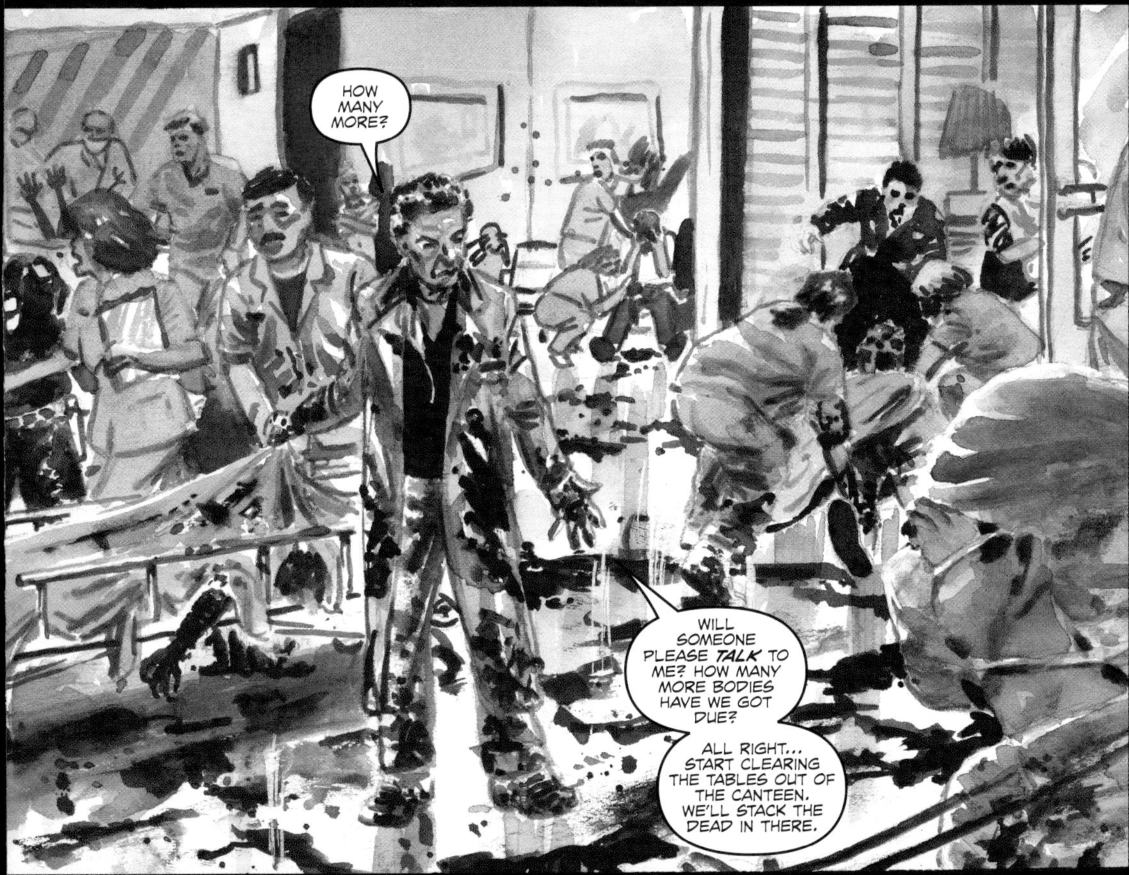
HOW MANY MORE?
WILL SOMEONE PLEASE *TALK* TO ME? HOW MANY MORE BODIES HAVE WE GOT DUE?
ALL RIGHT... START CLEARING THE TABLES OUT OF THE CANTEEN. WE'LL STACK THE DEAD IN THERE.

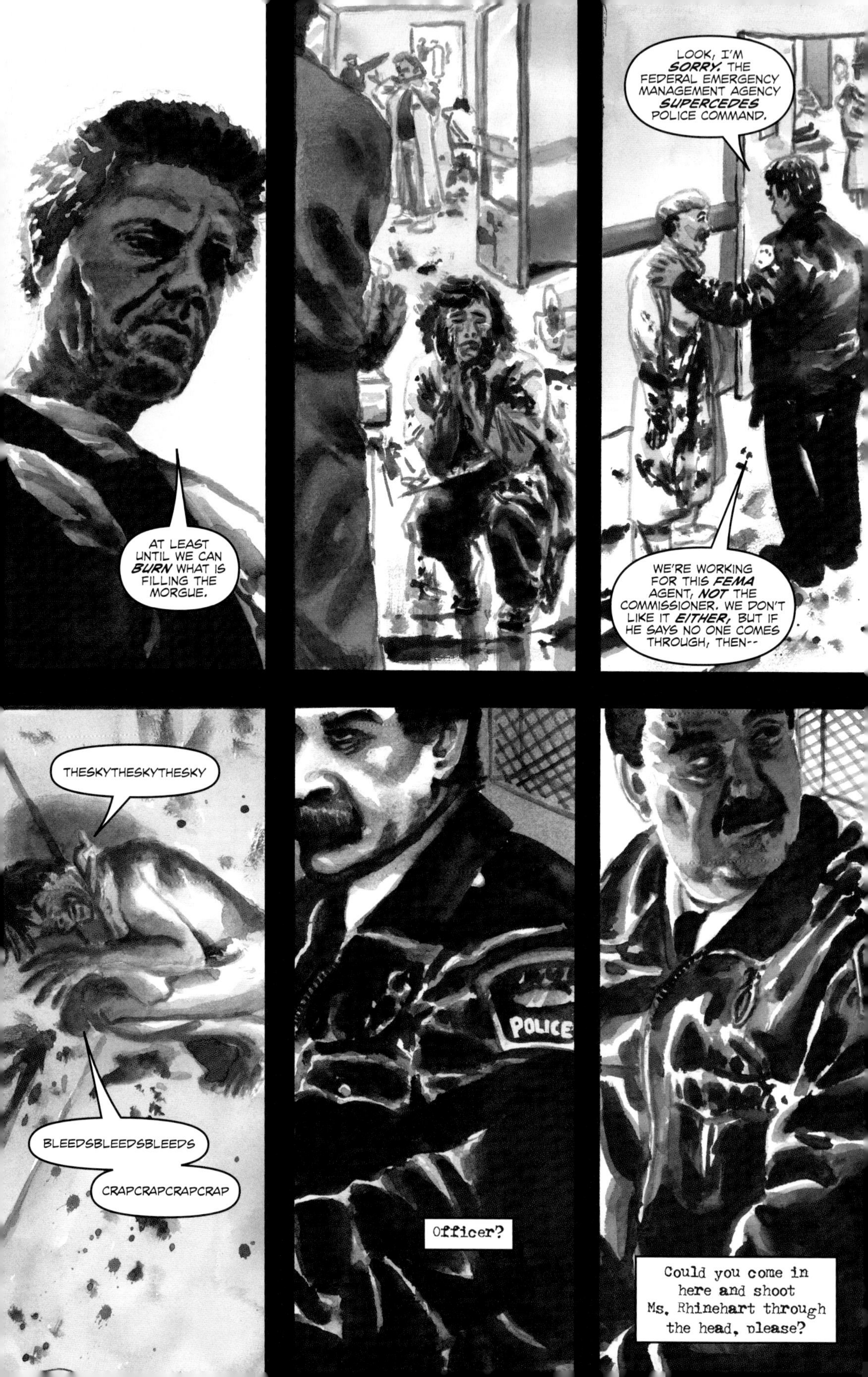
AT LEAST UNTIL WE CAN BURN WHAT IS FILLING THE MORGUE.
LOOK, I'M SORRY. THE FEDERAL EMERGENCY MANAGEMENT AGENCY SUPERCEDES POLICE COMMAND.
WE'RE WORKING FOR THIS FEMA AGENT, NOT THE COMMISSIONER. WE DON'T LIKE IT EITHER, BUT IF HE SAYS NO ONE COMES THROUGH, THEN--
THESKYTHESKYTHESKY
BLEEDSBLEEDSBLEEDS
CRAPCRAPCRAPCRAP
POLICE
Officer?
Could you come in here and shoot Ms. Rhinehart through the head, please?

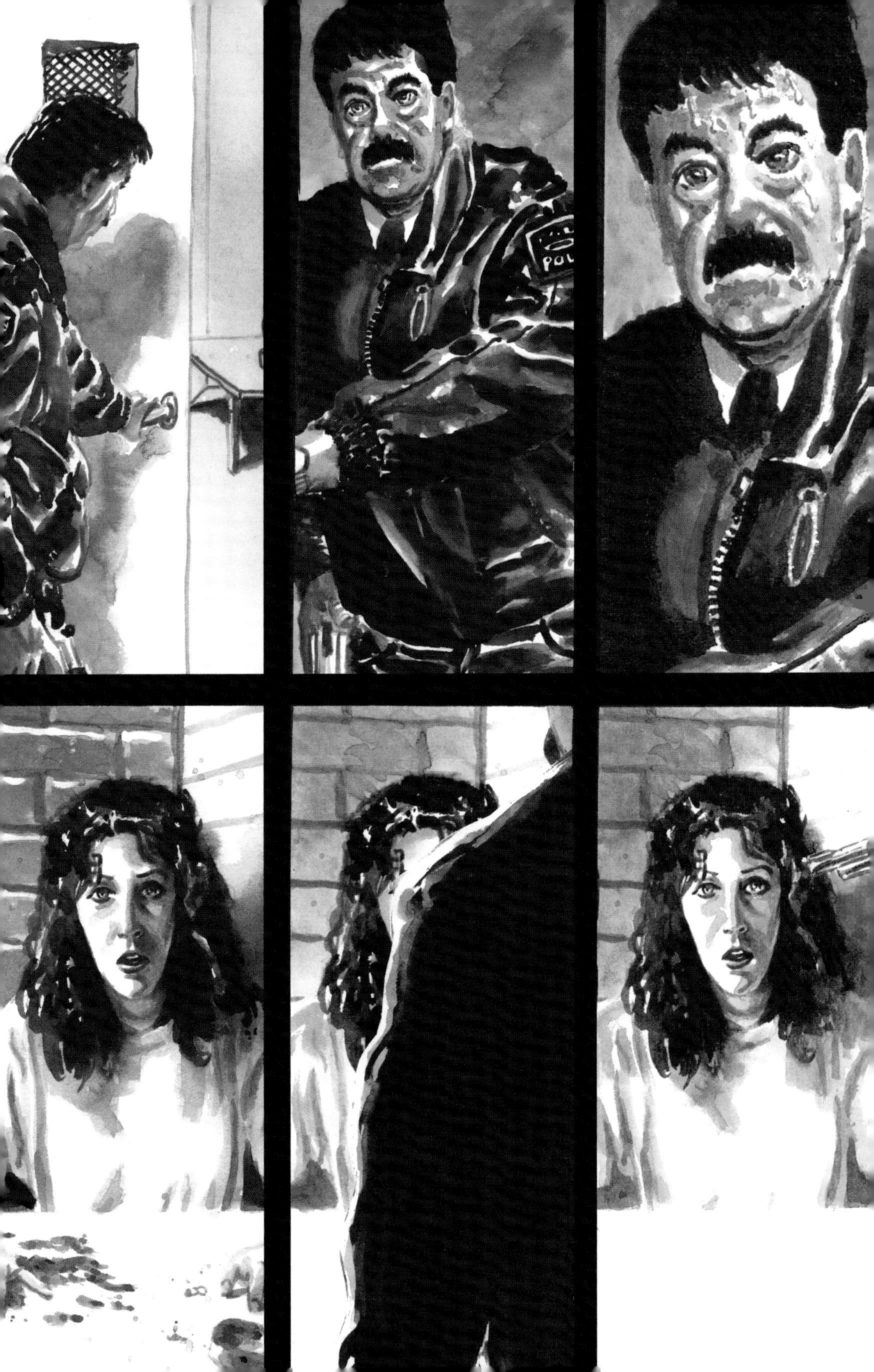

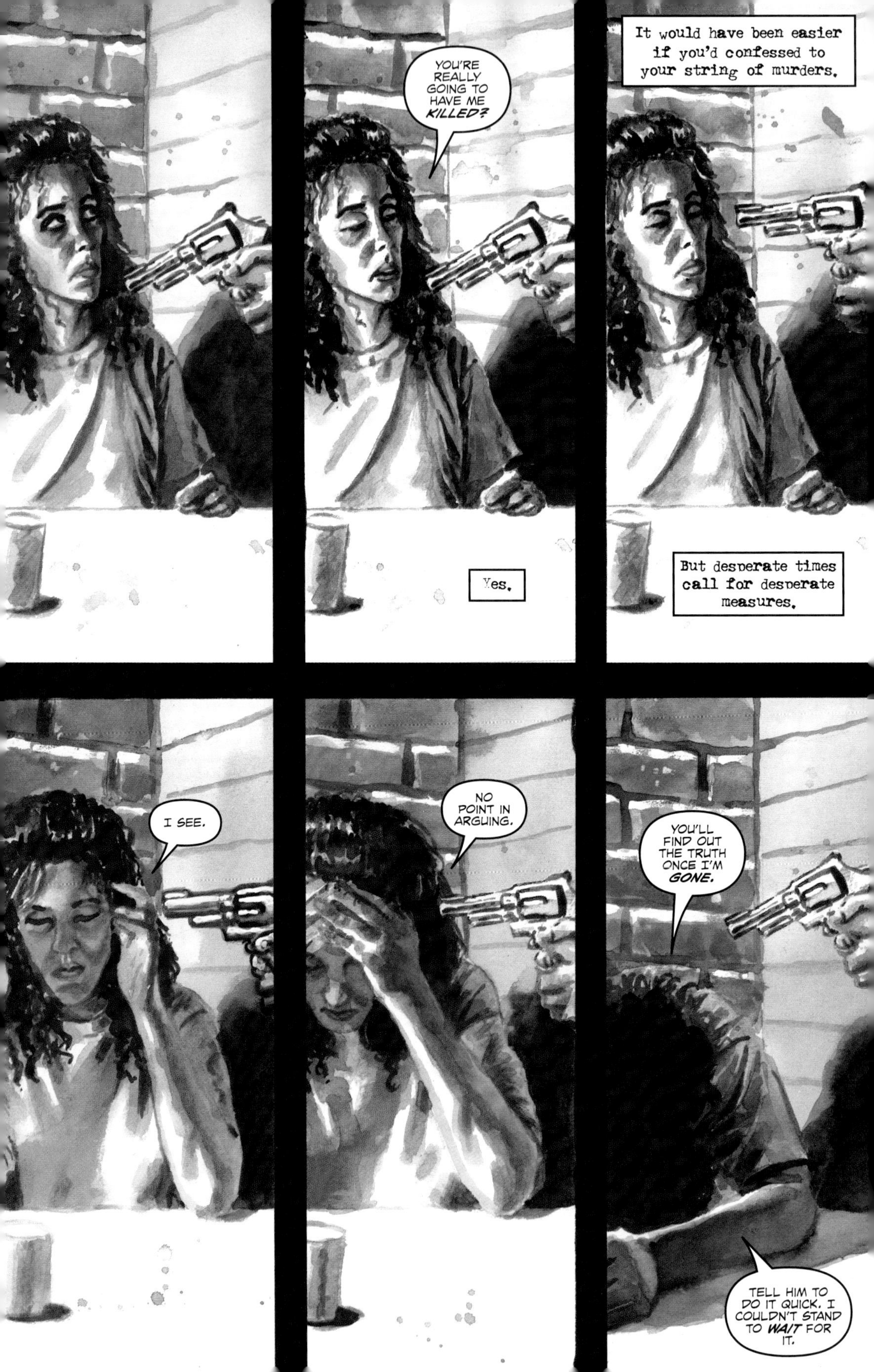
YOU'RE REALLY GOING TO HAVE ME KILLED?
Yes.
It would have been easier if you'd confessed to your string of murders.
But desperate times call for desperate measures.
I SEE.
NO POINT IN ARGUING.
YOU'LL FIND OUT THE TRUTH ONCE I'M GONE.
TELL HIM TO DO IT QUICK. I COULDN'T STAND TO WAIT FOR IT.

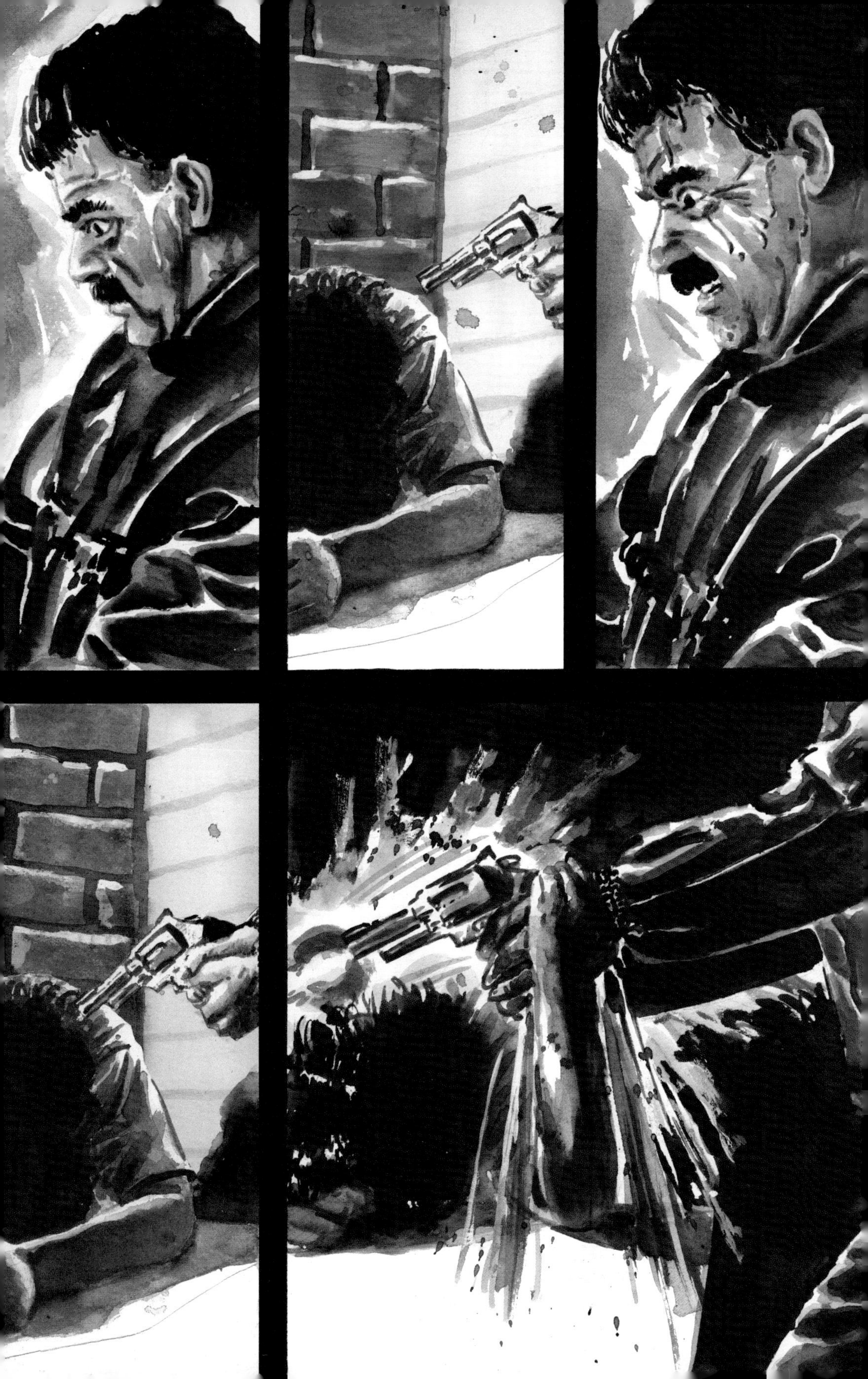

AAHHGGGGGK

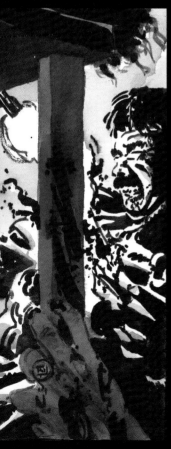

IT'S A GUT SHOT. YOU'LL LIVE FOR A WHILE YET.

WE'VE GOT TIME TO TALK.

Part Five

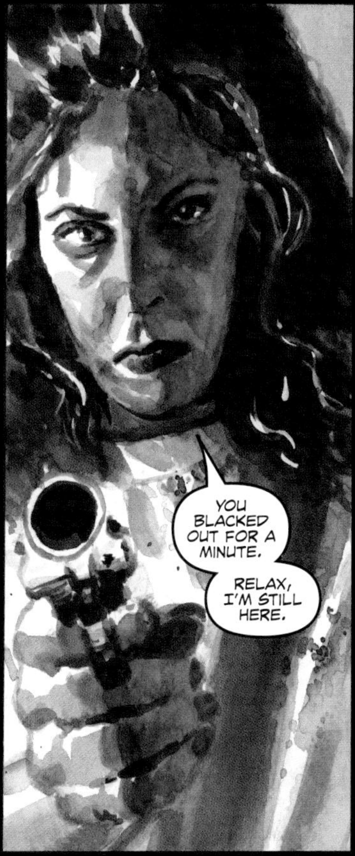
YOU BLACKED OUT FOR A MINUTE.
RELAX, I'M STILL HERE.

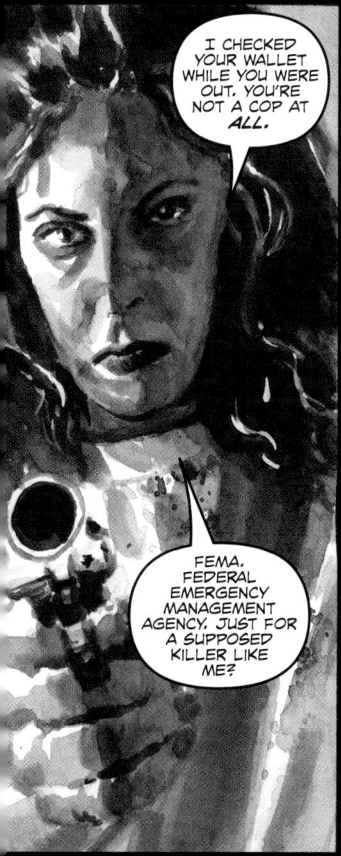
I CHECKED YOUR WALLET WHILE YOU WERE OUT. YOU'RE NOT A COP AT *ALL.*
FEMA. FEDERAL EMERGENCY MANAGEMENT AGENCY. JUST FOR A SUPPOSED KILLER LIKE ME?

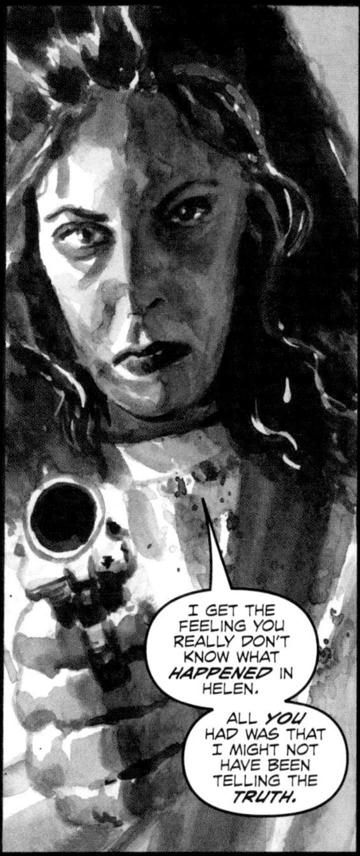
I GET THE FEELING YOU REALLY DON'T KNOW WHAT *HAPPENED* IN HELEN.
ALL *YOU* HAD WAS THAT I MIGHT NOT HAVE BEEN TELLING THE *TRUTH.*

WELL.

I WASN'T.

I'D HAD ENOUGH OF HELEN. TOO SMALL A PLACE; IT FELT LIKE I BARELY FIT *INSIDE* IT.

I STOLE A CAR. I DON'T *HAVE* A LICENSE. NEVER *TOOK* A TEST. AN OLD BOYFRIEND TAUGHT ME HOW TO DRIVE ONE SUMMER.

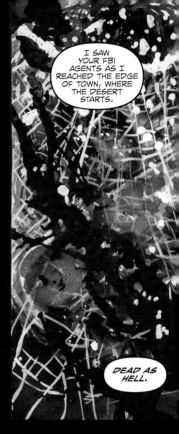

I SAW YOUR FBI AGENTS AS I REACHED THE EDGE OF TOWN, WHERE THE DESERT STARTS.

DEAD AS HELL.

ROAD WAS QUIET. I GOT OUT, CHECKED THE BODIES-- WENT THROUGH THEIR JACKETS FOR *MONEY,* TO BE *HONEST.*

FOUND THEIR I.D.

SAW THE CAR THAT'D DONE IT. THE CAR HAD SOMETHING INSIDE IT.

IT WAS SMALL AND GREY.

I DROVE BACK INTO TOWN AND DUMPED MY CAR. THE WHOLE THING GAVE ME THE *CREEPS.* I NEEDED A *DRINK.*

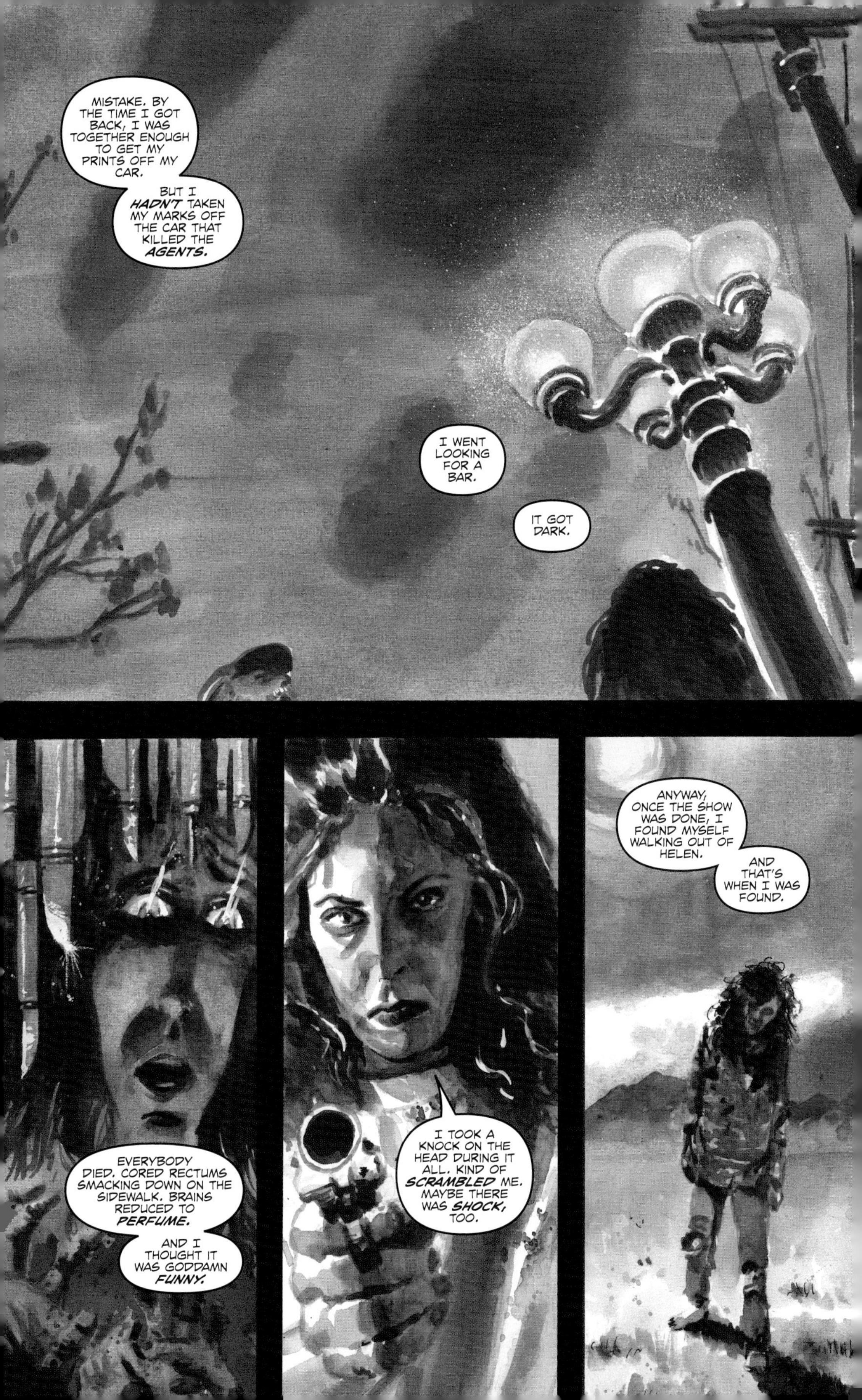
MISTAKE. BY THE TIME I GOT BACK, I WAS TOGETHER ENOUGH TO GET MY PRINTS OFF MY CAR.
BUT I *HADN'T* TAKEN MY MARKS OFF THE CAR THAT KILLED THE *AGENTS.*
I WENT LOOKING FOR A BAR.
IT GOT DARK.
EVERYBODY DIED. CORED RECTUMS SMACKING DOWN ON THE SIDEWALK. BRAINS REDUCED TO *PERFUME.*
AND I THOUGHT IT WAS GODDAMN *FUNNY.*
I TOOK A KNOCK ON THE HEAD DURING IT ALL. KIND OF *SCRAMBLED* ME. MAYBE THERE WAS *SHOCK,* TOO.
ANYWAY, ONCE THE SHOW WAS DONE, I FOUND MYSELF WALKING OUT OF HELEN.
AND THAT'S WHEN I WAS FOUND.

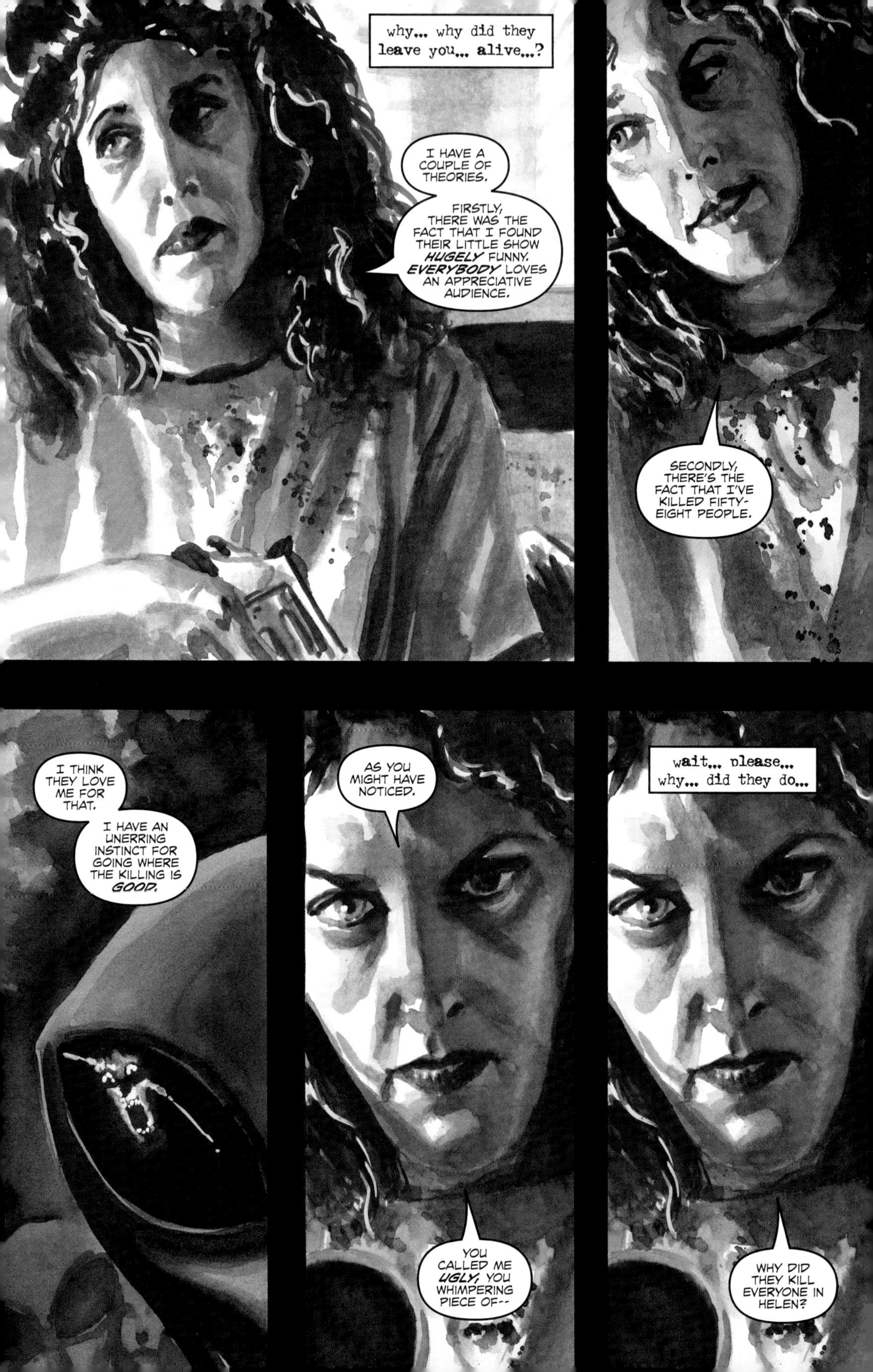
why... why did they leave you... alive...?
I HAVE A COUPLE OF THEORIES.
FIRSTLY, THERE WAS THE FACT THAT I FOUND THEIR LITTLE SHOW HUGELY FUNNY. EVERYBODY LOVES AN APPRECIATIVE AUDIENCE.
SECONDLY, THERE'S THE FACT THAT I'VE KILLED FIFTY-EIGHT PEOPLE.
I THINK THEY LOVE ME FOR THAT.
I HAVE AN UNERRING INSTINCT FOR GOING WHERE THE KILLING IS GOOD.
AS YOU MIGHT HAVE NOTICED.
YOU CALLED ME UGLY, YOU WHIMPERING PIECE OF--
wait... please... why... did they do...
WHY DID THEY KILL EVERYONE IN HELEN?

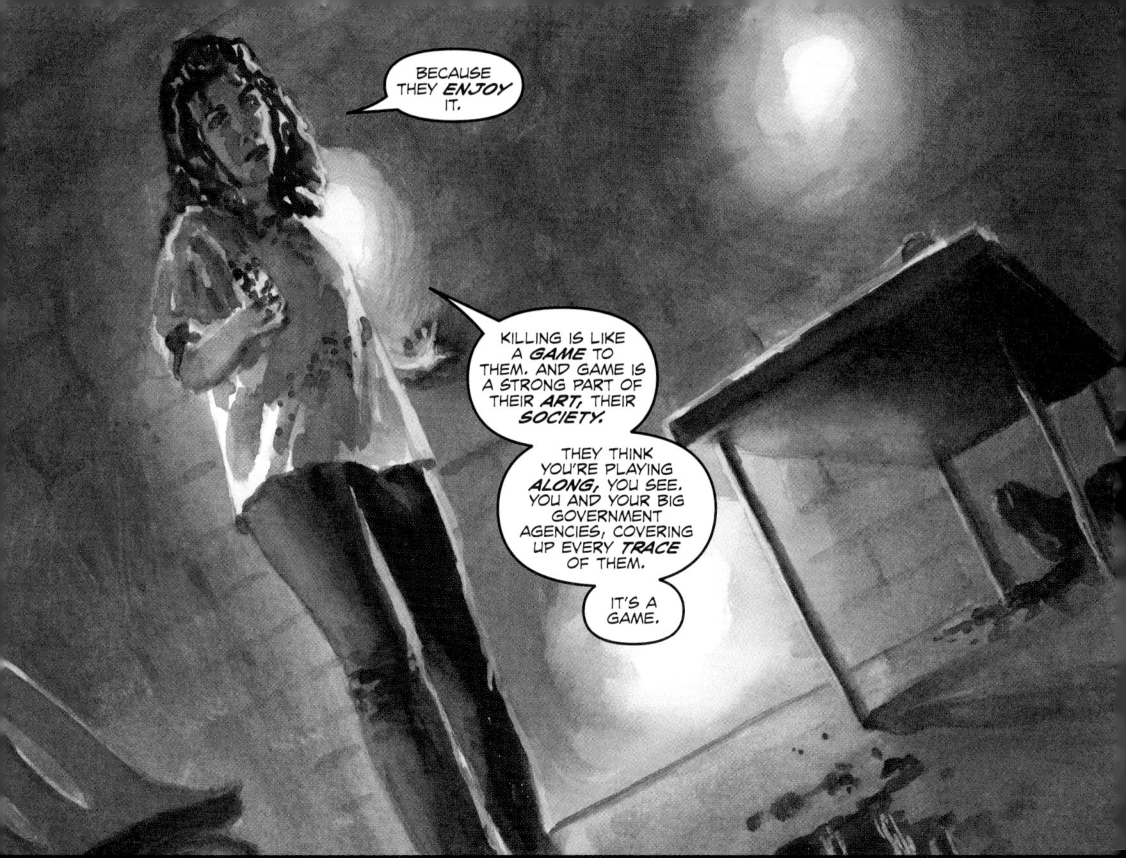
BECAUSE THEY ENJOY IT.
KILLING IS LIKE A GAME TO THEM. AND GAME IS A STRONG PART OF THEIR ART, THEIR SOCIETY.
THEY THINK YOU'RE PLAYING ALONG, YOU SEE. YOU AND YOUR BIG GOVERNMENT AGENCIES, COVERING UP EVERY TRACE OF THEM.
IT'S A GAME.

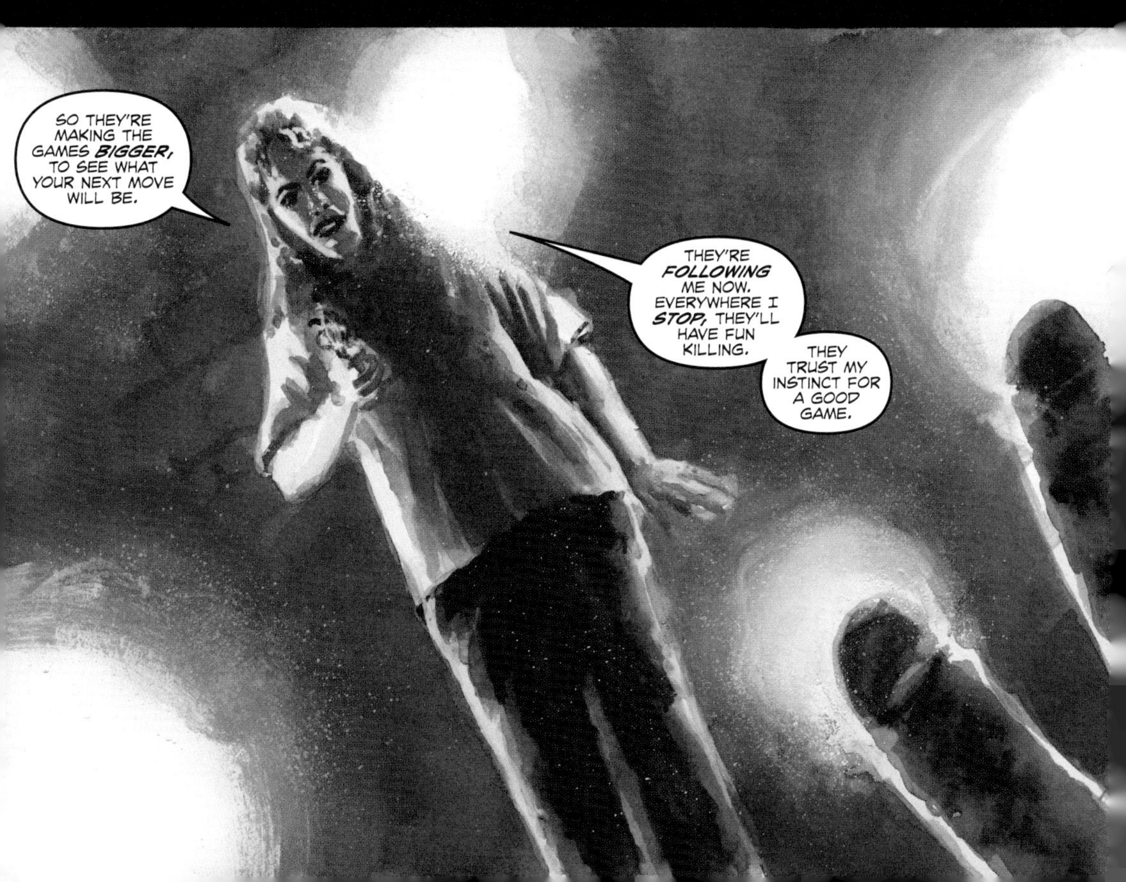
SO THEY'RE MAKING THE GAMES BIGGER, TO SEE WHAT YOUR NEXT MOVE WILL BE.
THEY'RE FOLLOWING ME NOW. EVERYWHERE I STOP, THEY'LL HAVE FUN KILLING.
THEY TRUST MY INSTINCT FOR A GOOD GAME.

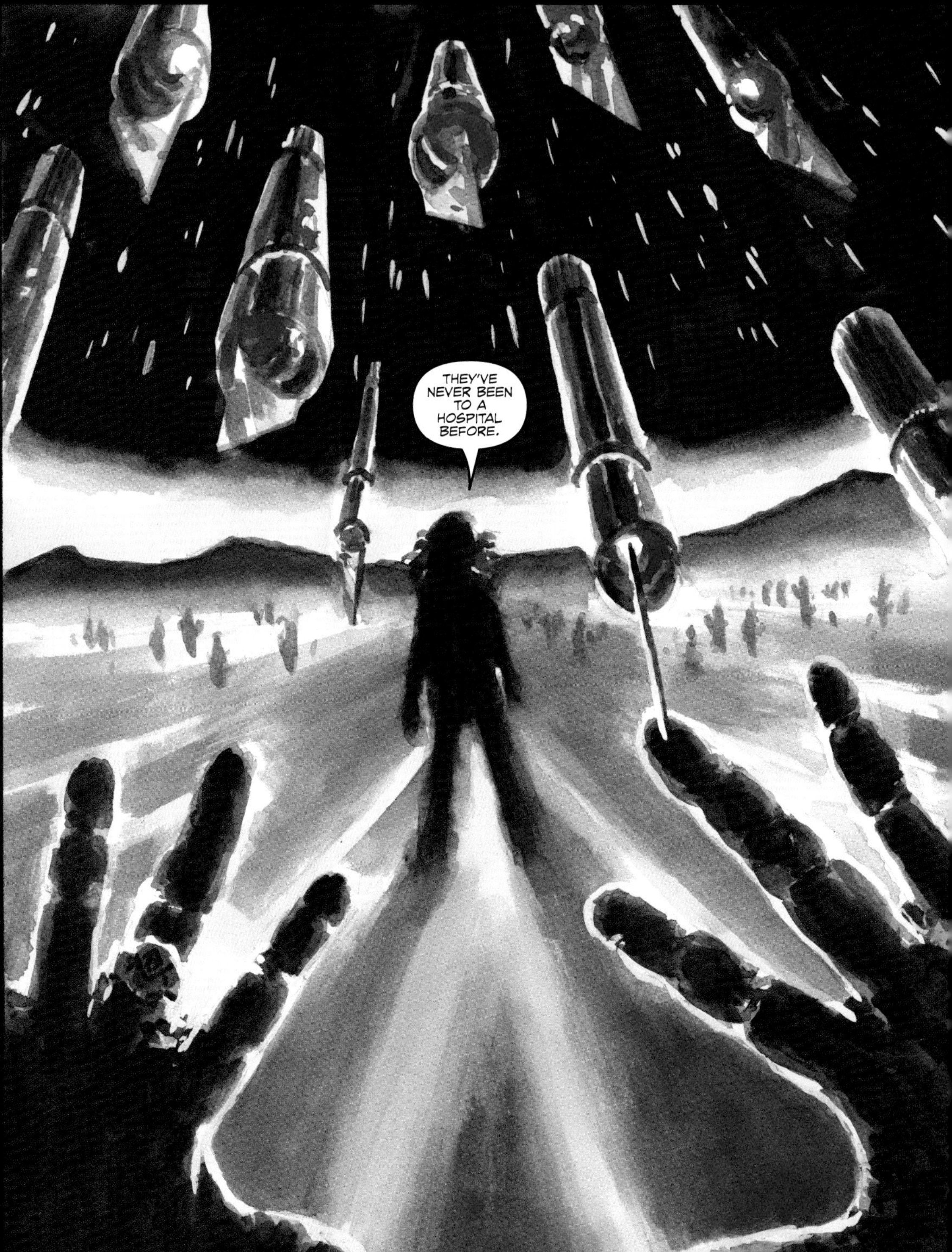
THEY'VE NEVER BEEN TO A HOSPITAL BEFORE.

End

AFTERWORD

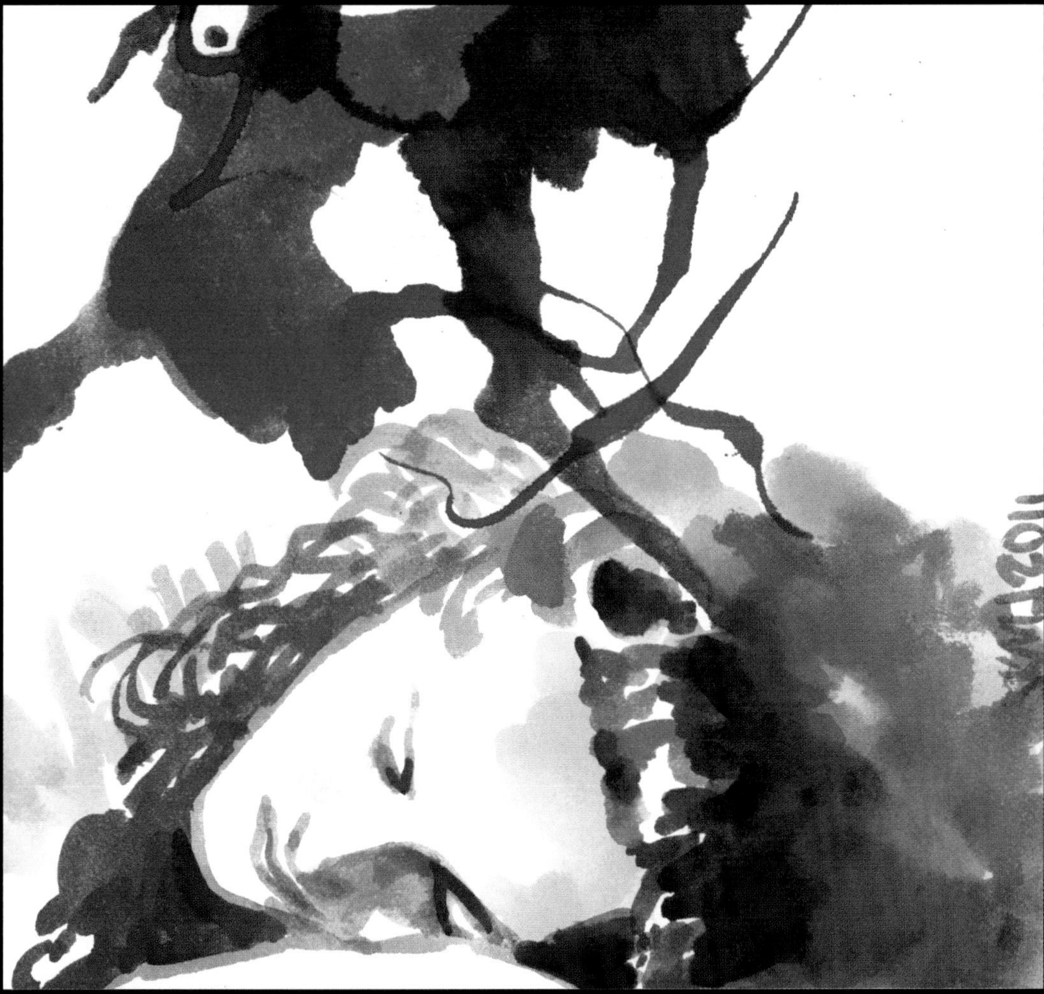

People say to me, where do you get your ideas from?

I get my ideas from being a bastard.

I don't believe in alien cattle mutilation. Not for a second. It's one of the dumber things the UFOlogist community has tried to palm off on the world over the last twenty years or so. And since we're also invited to believe that aliens would develop fantastic technology and travel incredible distances just to stick metal things up Whitley Streiber's arse, that's saying something. (As Robert Anton Wilson observed, "Maybe he's got the most adorable bum in the galaxy, but somehow I doubt that.")

I mean, we've come up with workable theories for mysteries such as the Stonehenge design, which was made by creatures whose brains were wired significantly differently to ours, but I've yet to see a compelling explanation for alien mutilation of cattle. So, you know, I'm not taking this "They're aliens, of course we don't understand their thinking" argument on. What do aliens need a cow's cored-out arsehole for? Are you telling me that they can develop magical propulsion systems but can't clone cows? We can clone sheep and my girlfriend's car rattles like buggery if she tries pushing it past eighty. I'm not convinced. Are Earth cow arses especially delicious? Can the particular flavour of Earth cowguts not be replicated by their evil Strieber-poking science? Are their engines powered by cow arses? Are these mutilations the result of a refueling stop on the way to Whitley Strieber's house?

(I shouldn't take the piss out of Strieber, a man with a documented weakness for religion, whom I believe is genuinely ill. But, you know– it's funny.)

All these things happen in banjo country, and are usually reported by people half-blind from moonshine saying that there are strange bright lights in the sky when it happens that have nothing at all to do with the neighbours dynamiting Cousin Betty Mae for looking at a black man. You've seen DELIVERANCE. You know what's being covered up when a bull is having an orifice cut out. You know that someone, somewhere, is muttering darkly that the bull was a slut and deserved everything it got.

But.

I spent a night reading through post-mortem reports of mutilated cattle. I read odd stuff sometimes. A big part of this game is reading

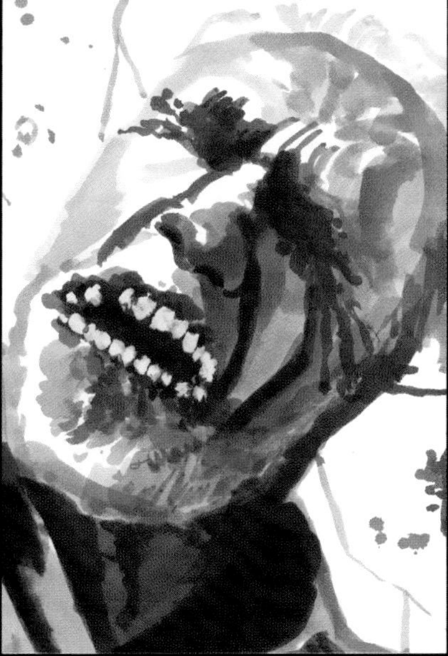

as much as possible, filling up your brain with it and letting it all fuse together until it turns into a story. I'm sitting here reading this disgusting shit, drinking and smoking and just letting it all pour in... and then I have this thought.

"Why don't they do this to people?"

I mean, if you for a moment choose to accept that alien beings travel across the galaxy just to fuck with us (while producing no radio signals at all ever, apparently)... this is a two-birds-with-one-stone situation, surely.

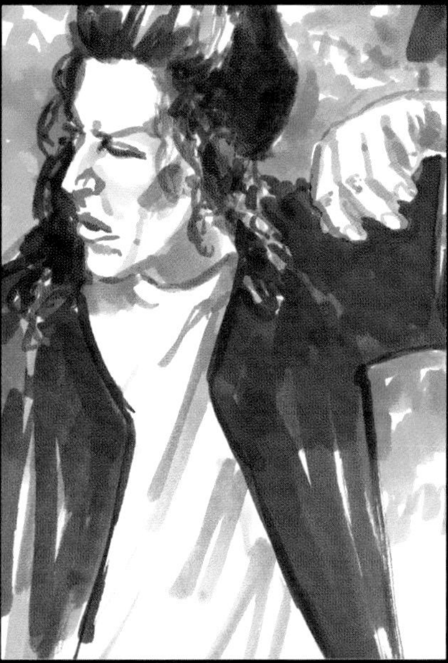

Take the arses with you to probe all you like.

Just hack 'em out, stick 'em in your bag, and you're off. Hours of playing poke-the-bum at your complete leisure, in the comfort of your own flying saucer.

"Evening, Whitley. We've had enough of the commute from Zeta Reticuli to your place every Friday night. So tonight we're chopping your arse off and taking it with us. Bend over, there's a good lad."

I sat down and rewrote one of the autopsy reports to reflect a human body instead of a cow carcass.

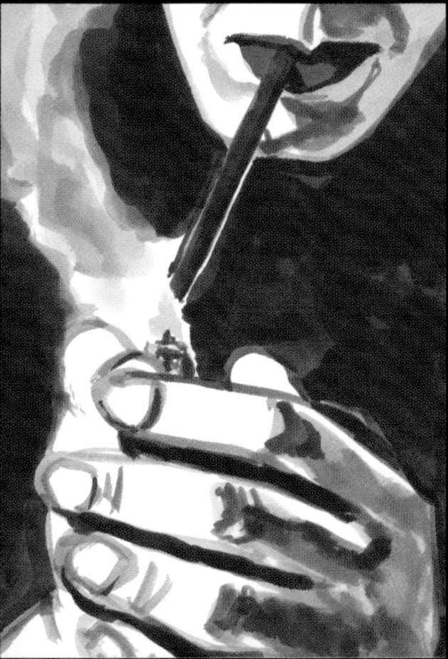

This was a genuinely horrible idea, inspired by nothing but a spirit of meanness in considering a man I've never met and who has never harmed me or anyone I know.

So I wrote it.

Don't live with writers. Writers are bastards.

Warren Ellis
Southend
April 2002

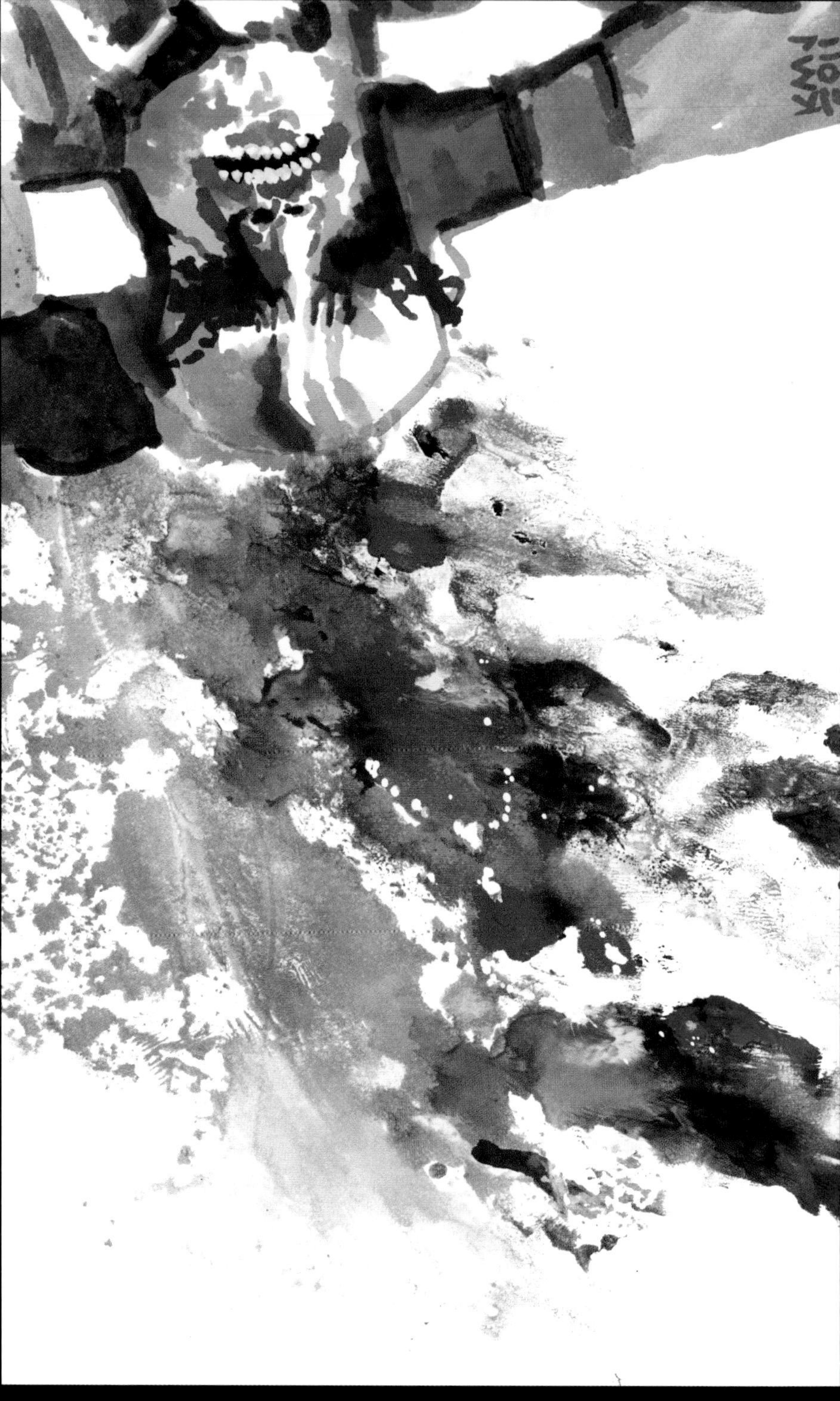

ATMOSPHERICS SKETCH GALLERY

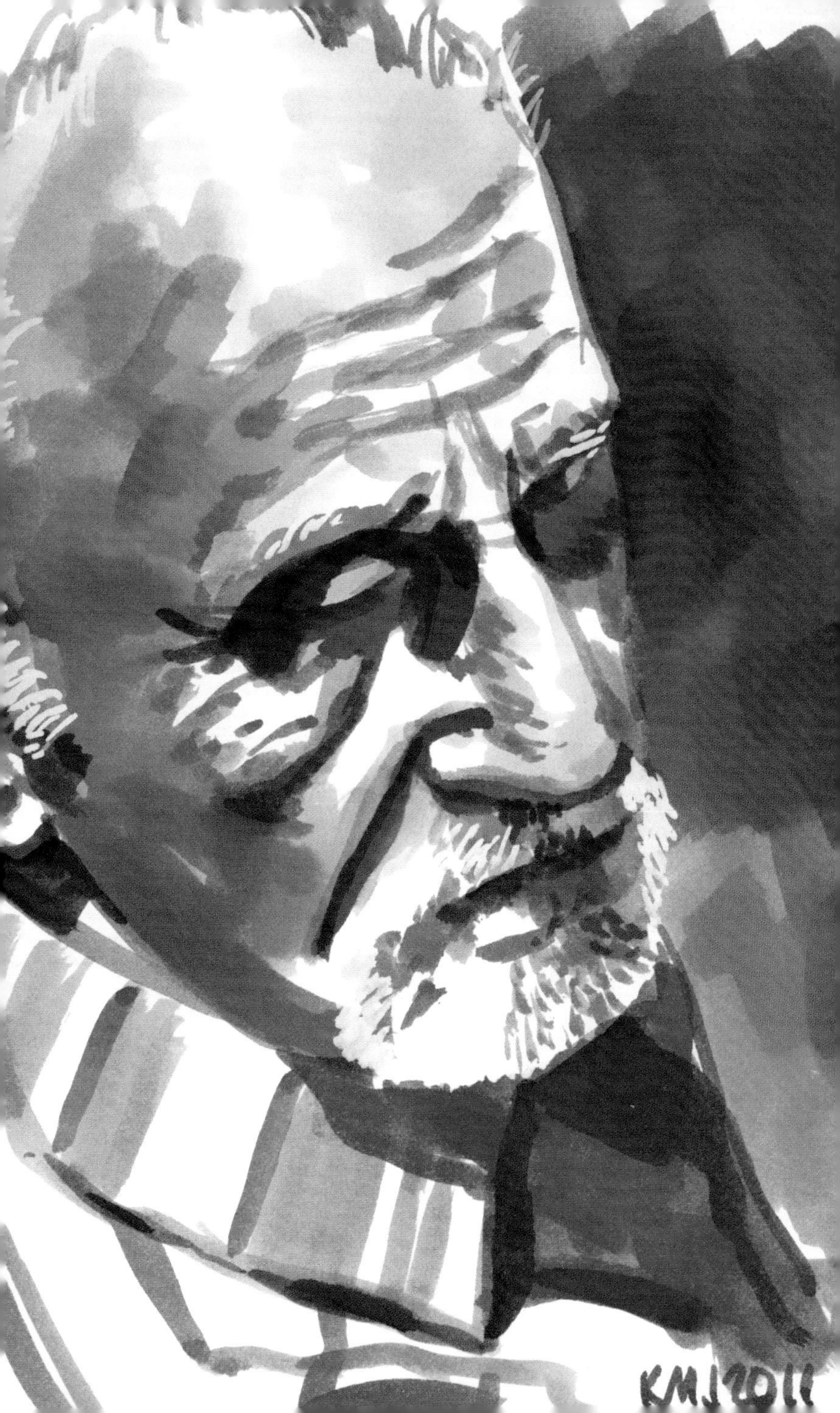
KMJ 2011

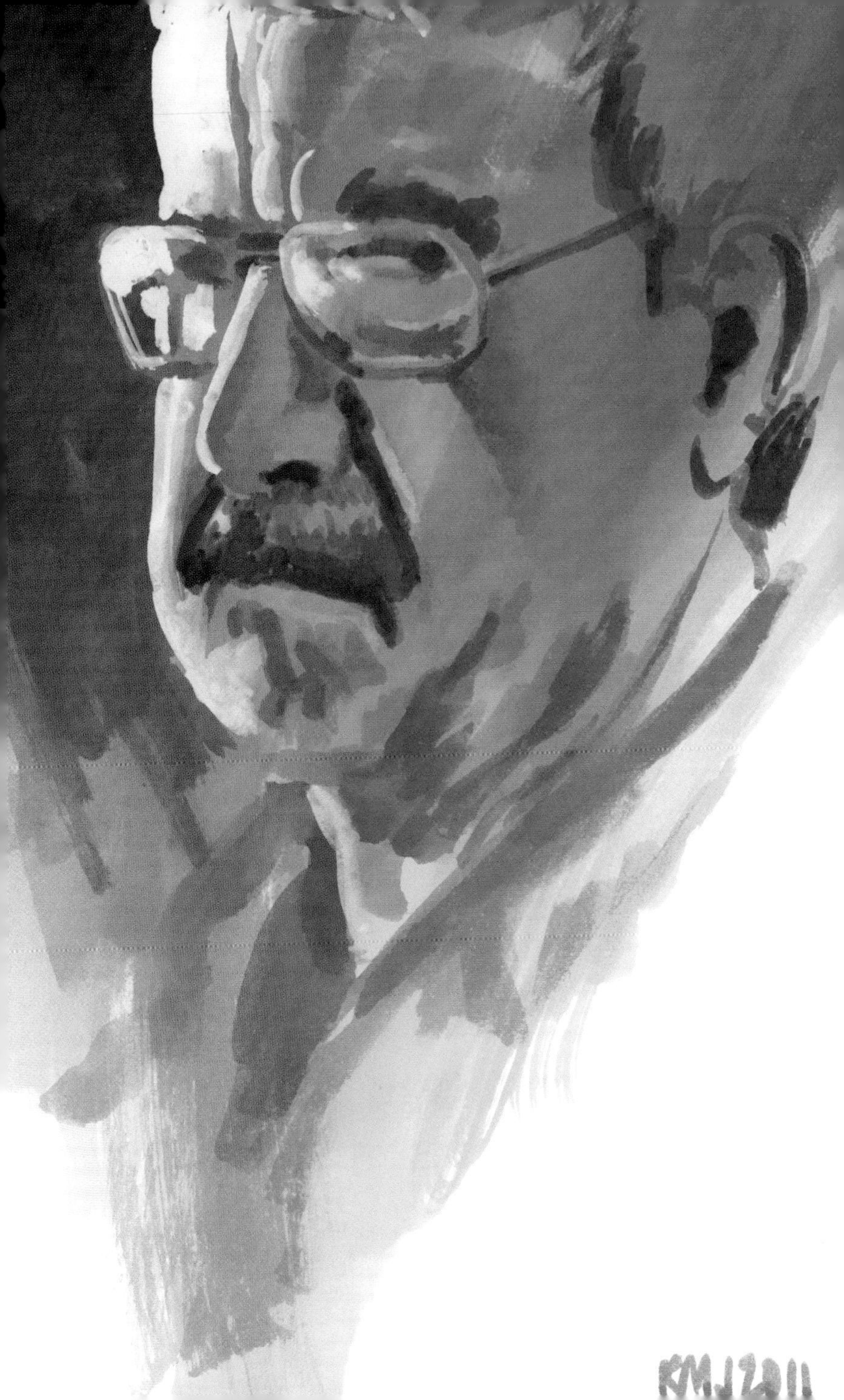
KMJ2011

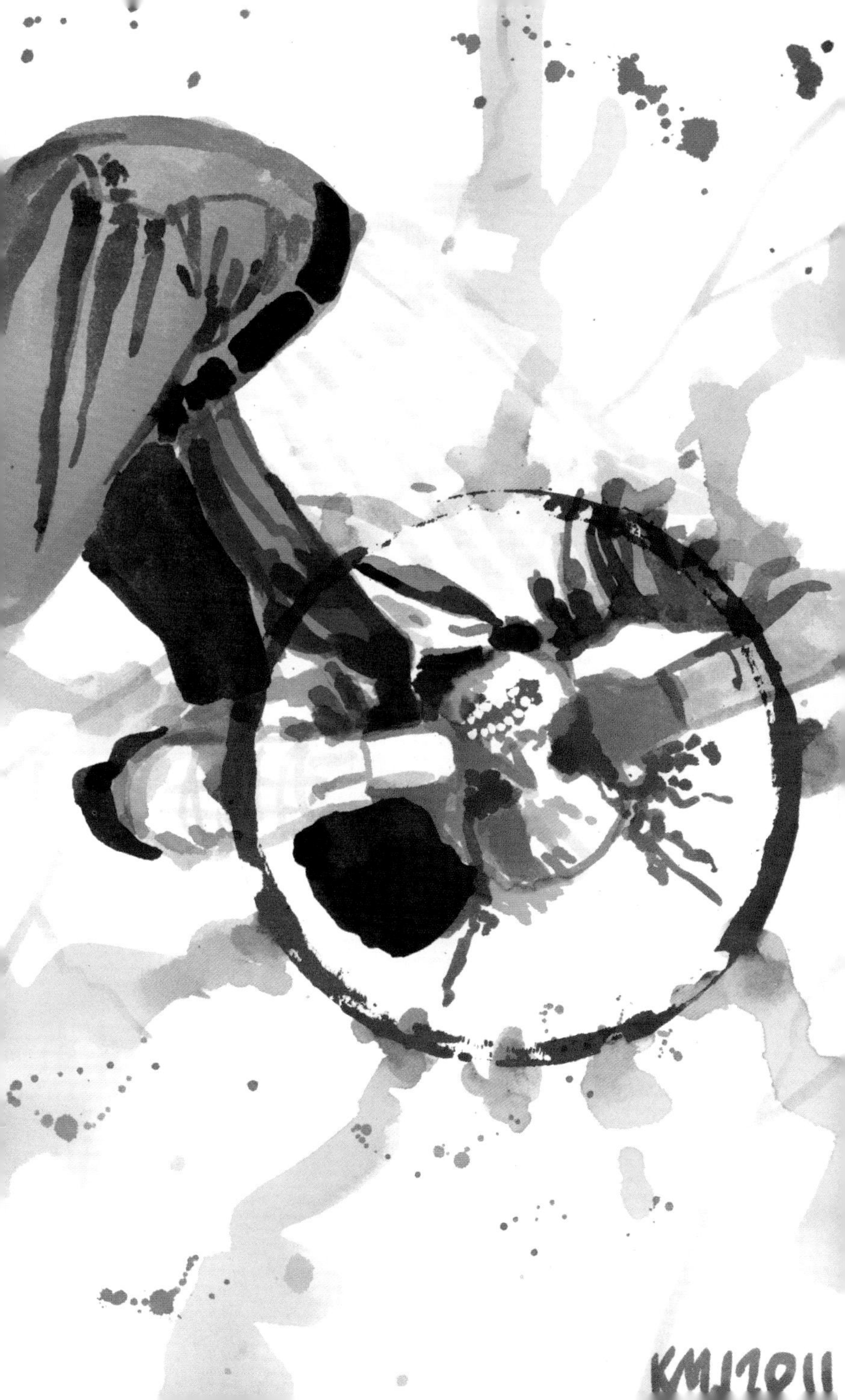
KMJ2011

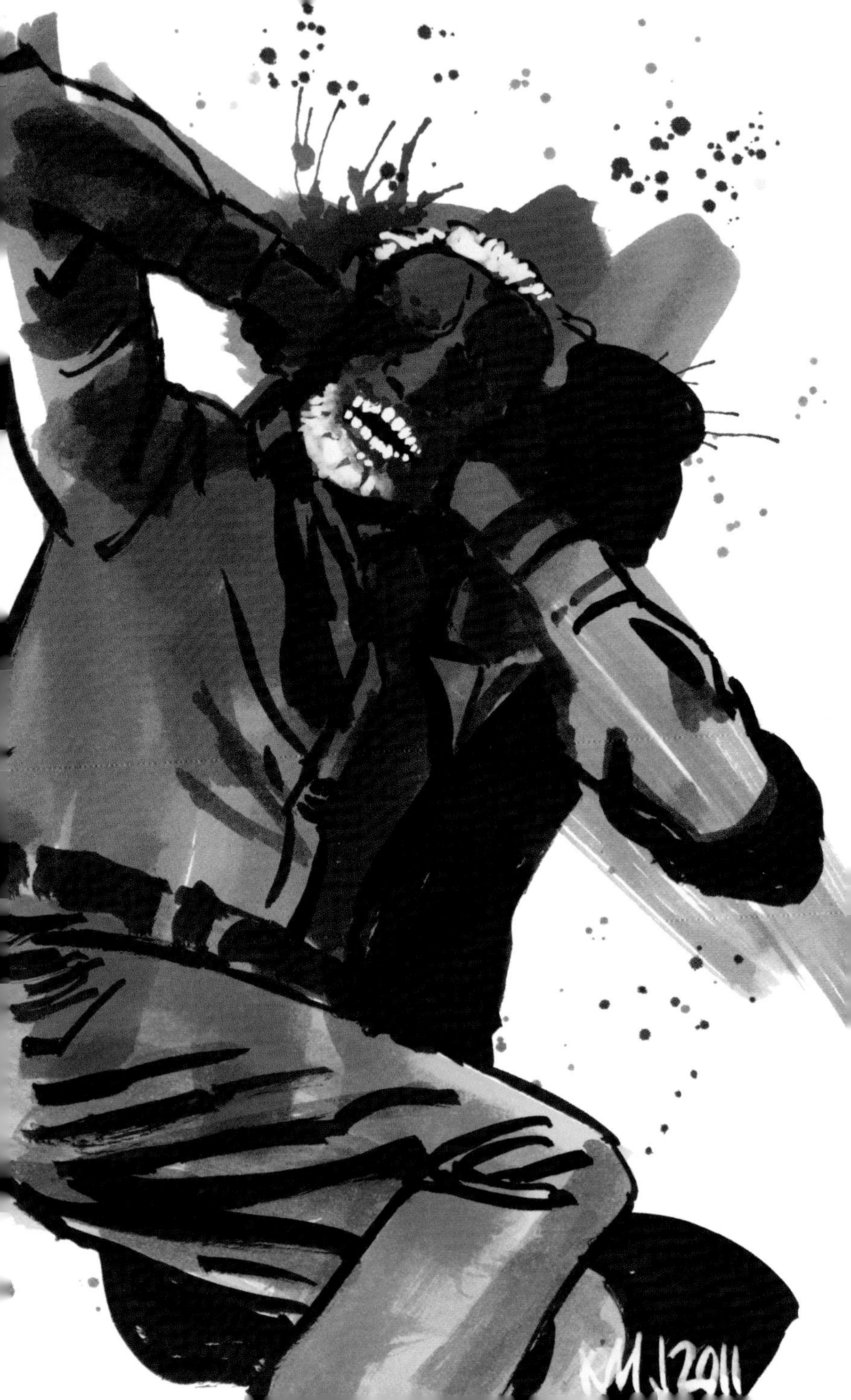
KMJ 2011

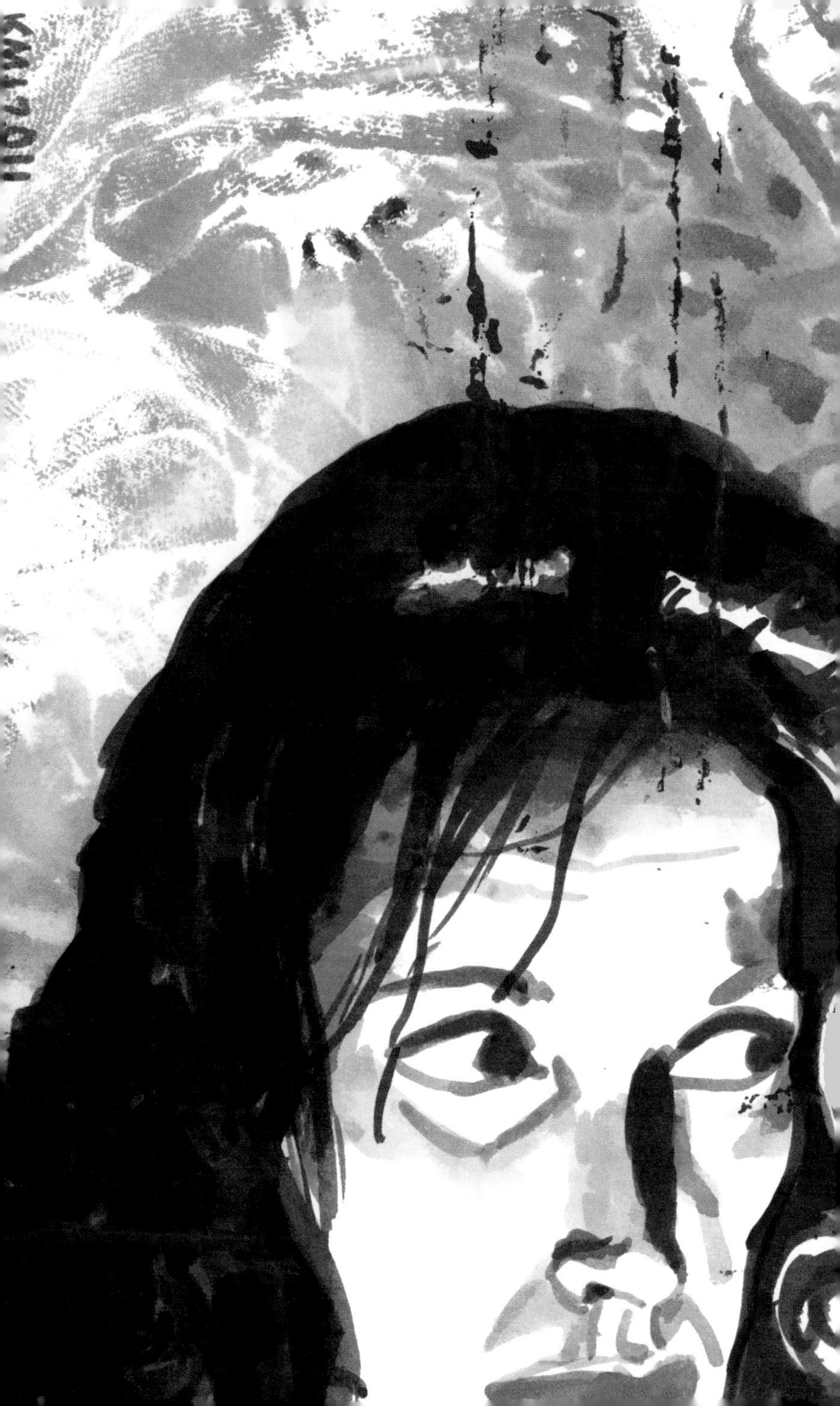

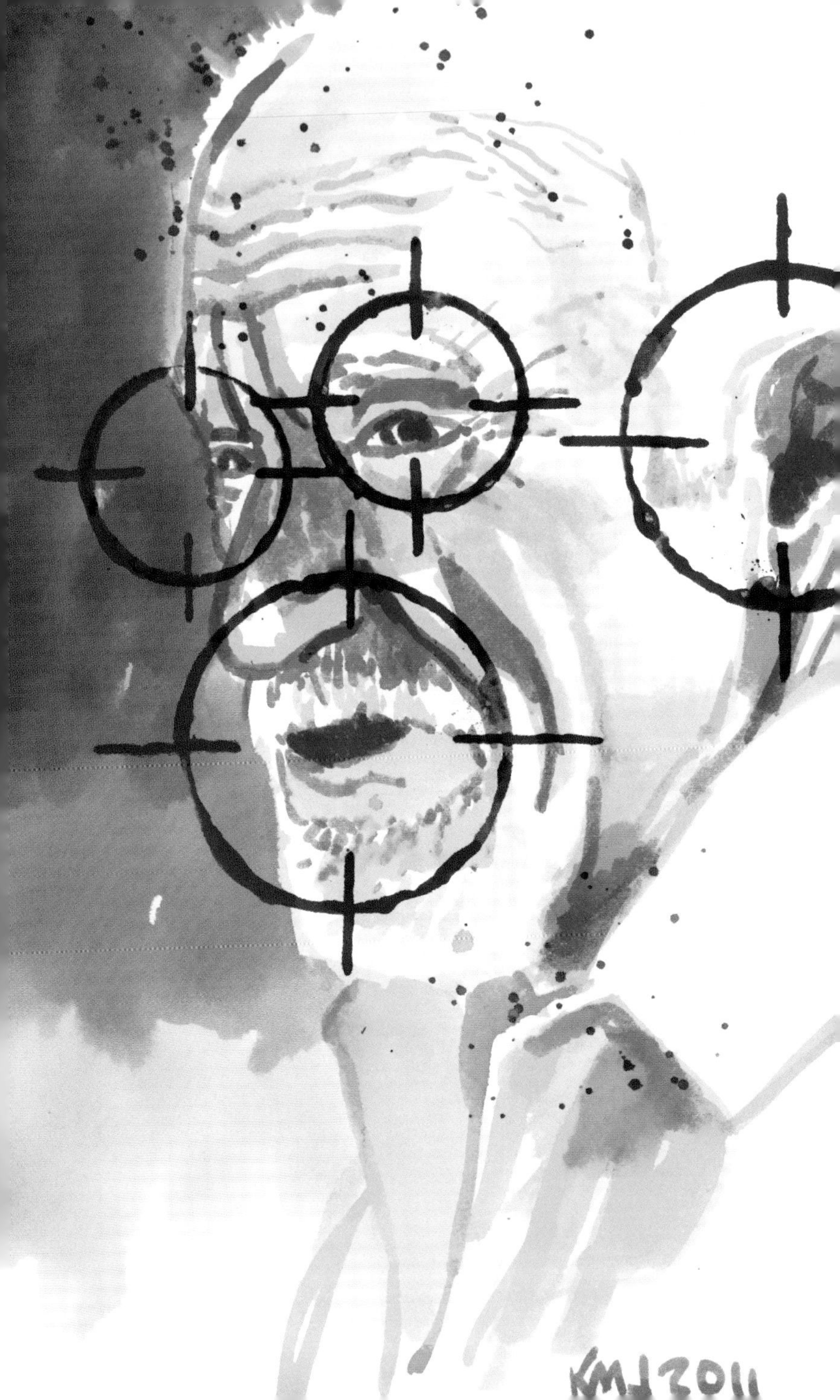
KMJ 2011

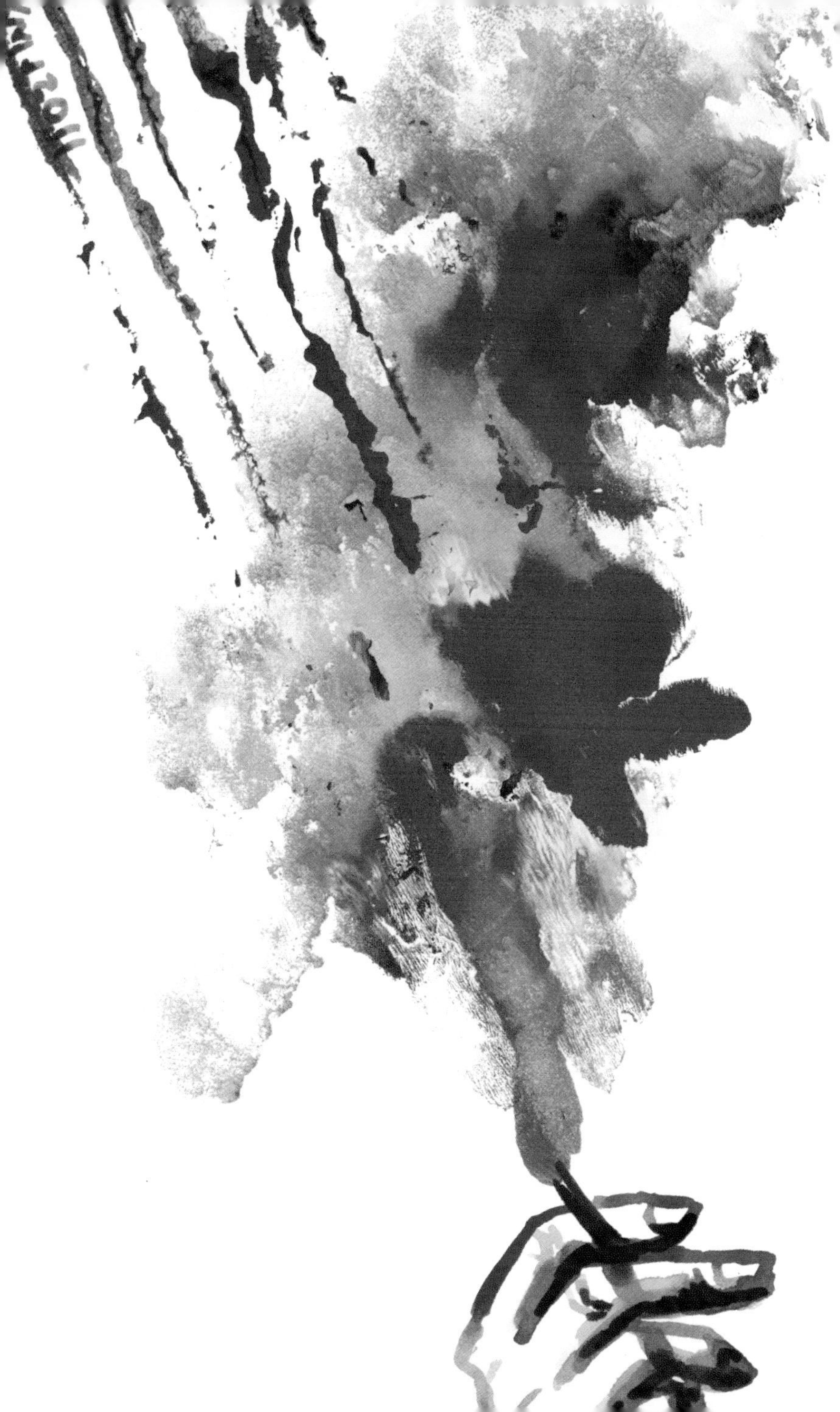

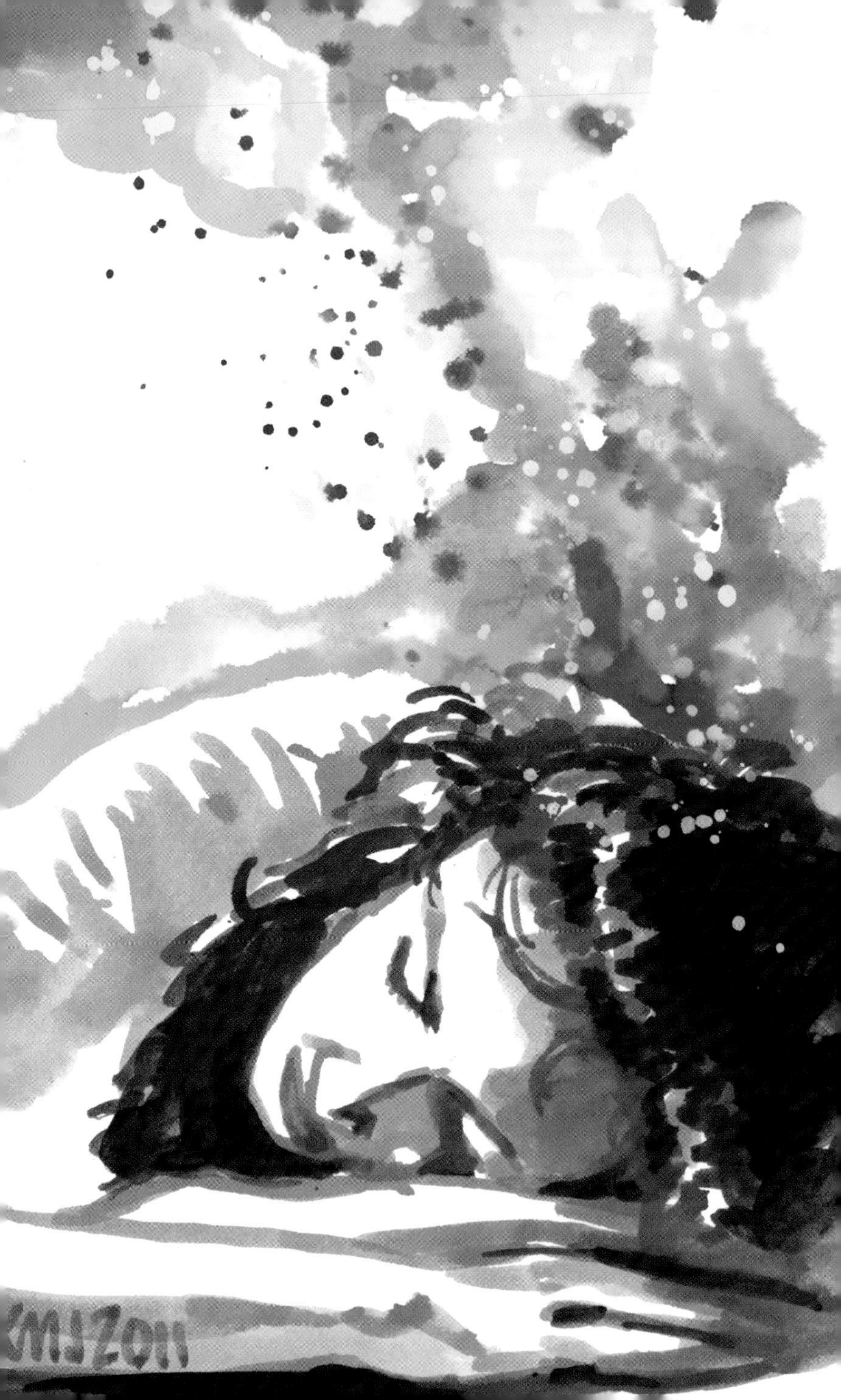

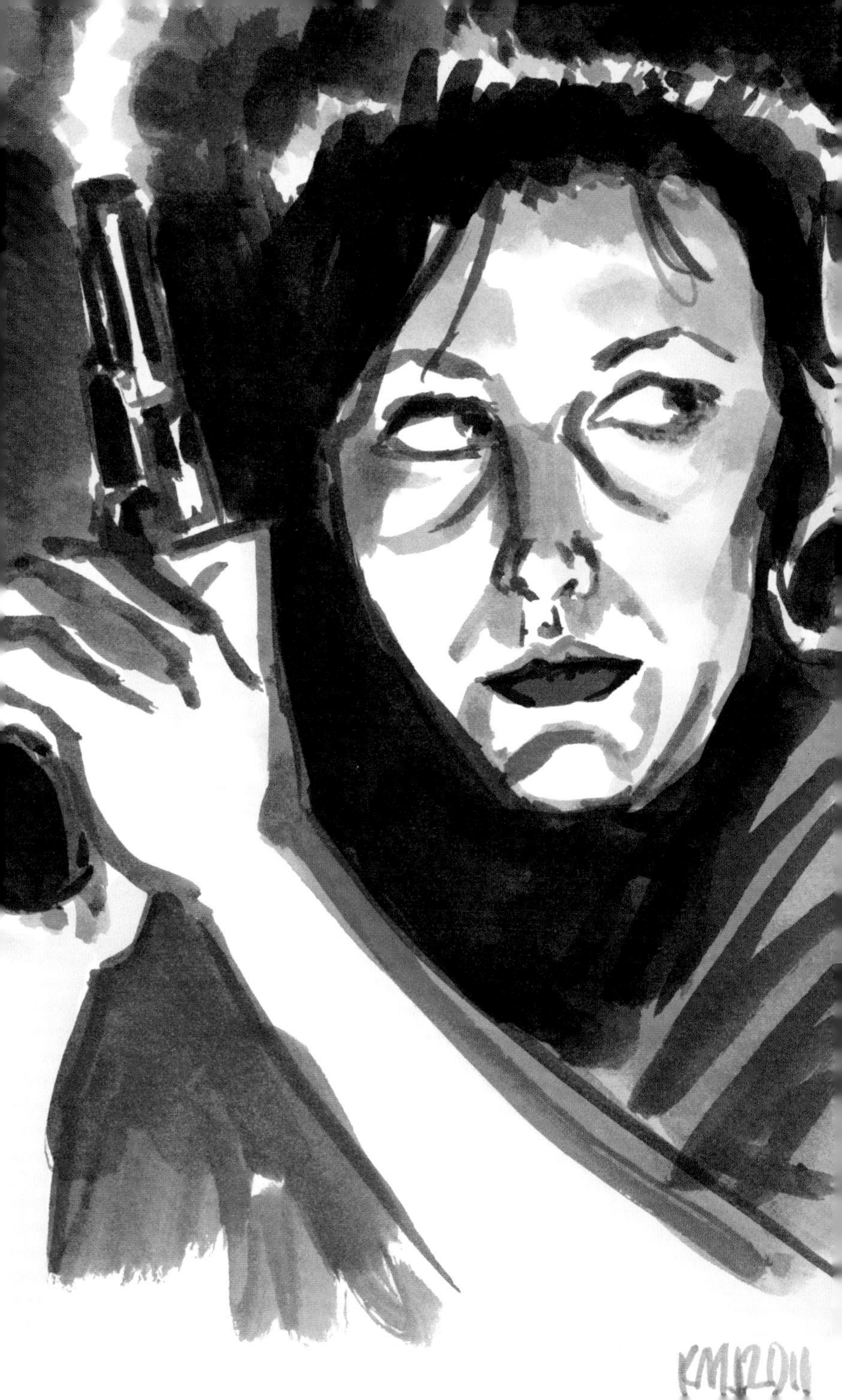

KM12011

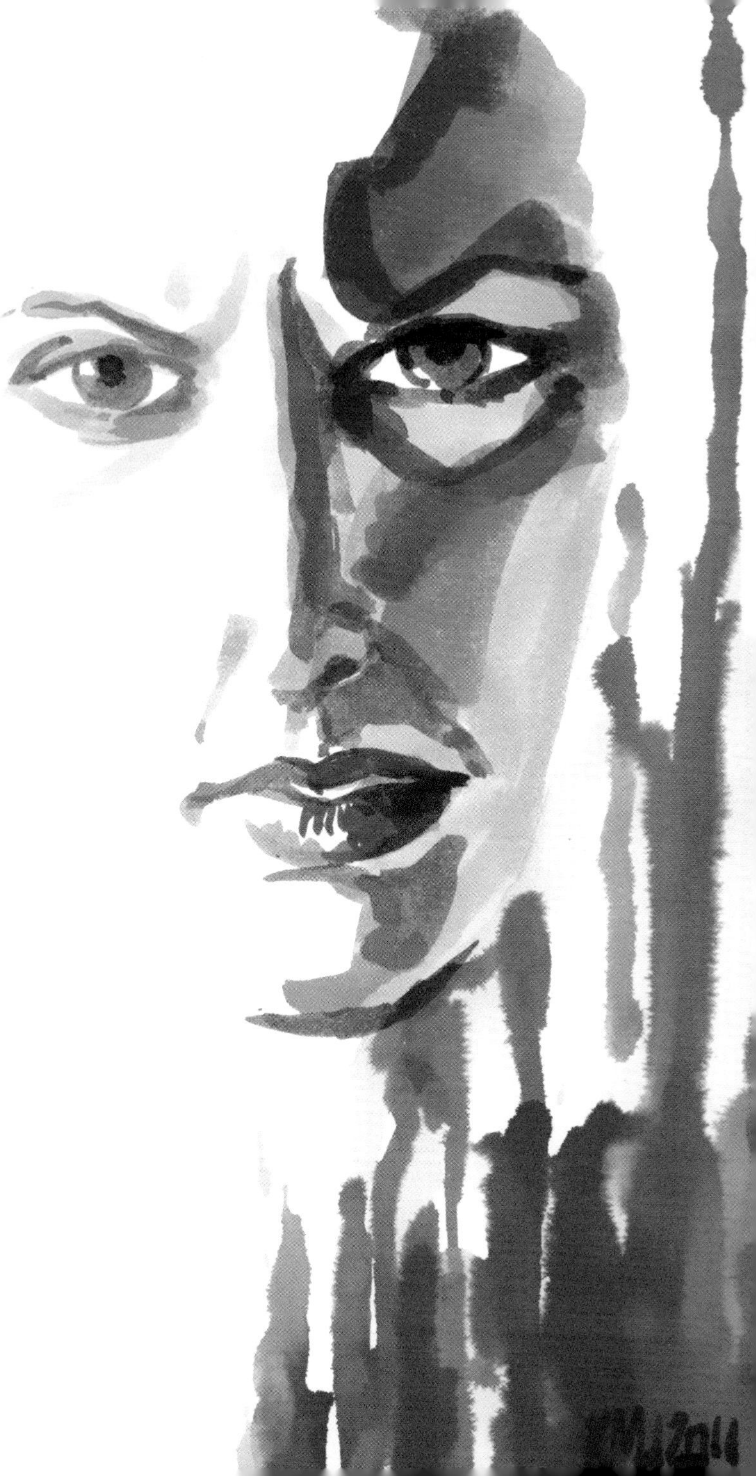

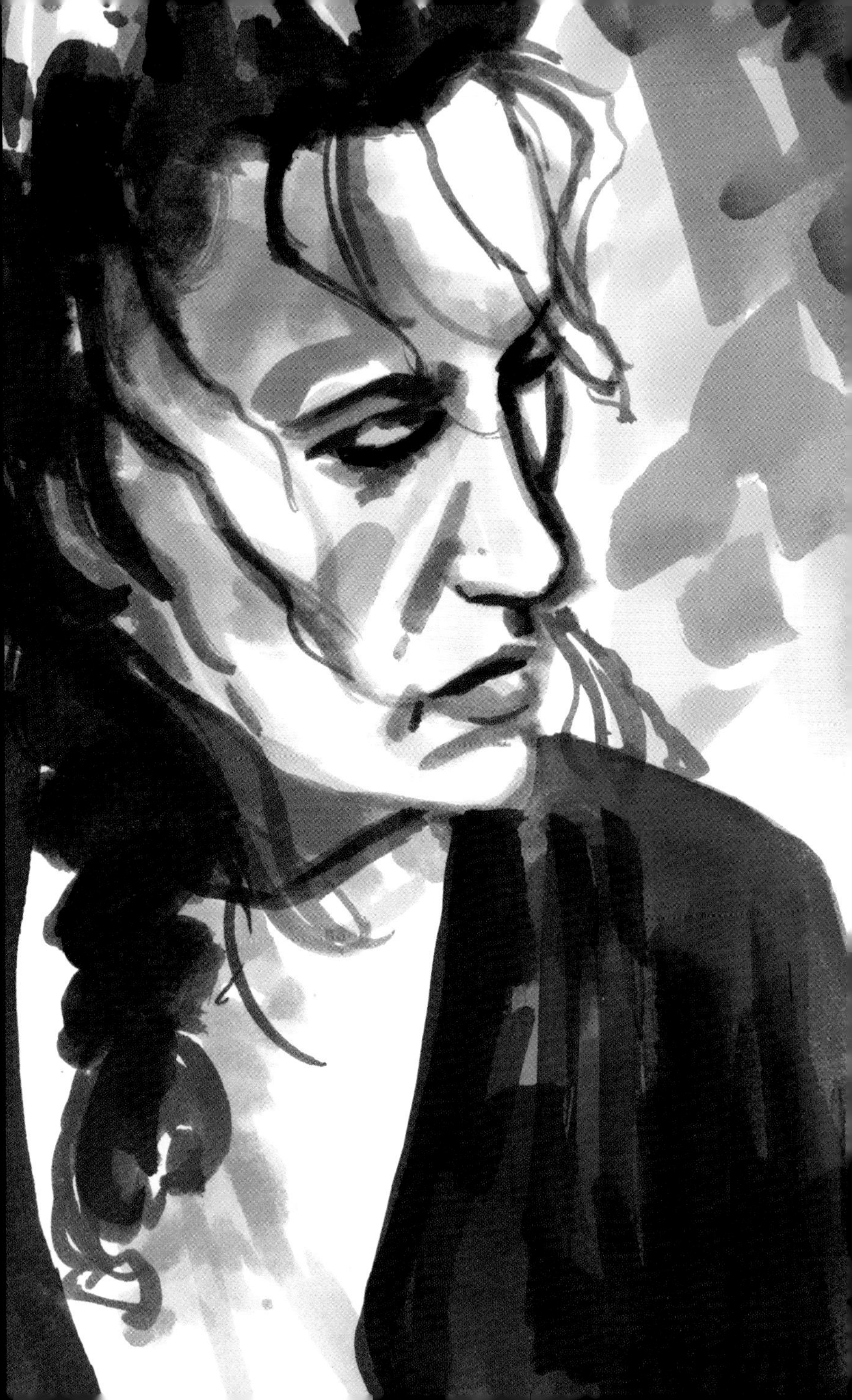